May you go from strength
to strength

Michael Bradfeld
Cheryl Enin

BUT SOME BECAME STARS

Susi Bradfield

[With John Burns]

gefen publishing house

JERUSALEM ◆ NEW YORK

Typesetting: Marzel A.S. – Jerusalem
Cover Design: Studio Paz, Jerusalem

Edition   9   8   7   6   5   4   3   2

Gefen Publishing House Ltd.   Gefen Books
POB 36004   12 New Street
Jerusalem 91360, Israel   Hewlett, NY 11557, USA
972-2-5380247   516-295-2805
E-mail: isragefen@netmedia.net.il

Printed in Israel
Send for our free catalogue

Library of Congress Cataloging-in-Publication Data
Bradfield, Susi, 1929-
But some became stars / Susi Bradfield with John Burns.
     p.   cm.
ISBN: 965 229 193 5
1. Bradfield, Susi, 1929- . 2. Jews—Germany—Berlin—Biography. 3. Jews, German—
England—Biography. 4. Refugees, Jewish— England—Biography. 5. Berlin (Germany)—
Biography. 6. Berlin (Germany)— Ethnic relations. [1. Germany—History—1933-1945.]
I. Burns, John. II. Title.
DS135.G5B67 1998
943'.155004924'00922—dc21
[b]   98-35803
                                                                CIP

To my beloved grandchildren - Gabrielle and Matthew, and Marco and Miriel; to the children and grandchildren of my sister Paula, and of my brothers Siche and Myer; and to the children and future grandchildren of my brothers-in-law Ernie and Paul.

Contents

How It Began...

When we were very young, every Friday evening around the dinner table Papa would tell us stories; true life stories.

They had the quality of folk tales, yet these were part of our family history, passed down from parent to child the way it had always been.

When I became a grandmother I resolved that I too would take up the family tradition.

But the dinner table of these days is very different from the days of my own childhood. Now it is often a noisy forum for everyone's views and frequently the stories were cut short as the conversation veered off down some other avenue.

So I thought I should write a book instead.

At first the idea was little more than a passing fancy. Then I began to think seriously about it. Where should this book begin – with the saga of my own childhood flight from the Nazis? Or perhaps the mystery of who shot the SS man? Or again the tale of what we did in the Six Day War?

As I mused over my memories I came to realise these were stories not just for my grandchildren. So much of our past is interwoven with the darkest era of this century; a time when the history of millions of other families came to a brutal full stop. Yet we were spared. That simple fact decided me that yes, I would write a book, for it is a story that must not be lost.

But it took a sharply poignant reminder of our own good fortune to make me take up my pen.

THE ICE CREAM
MOUNTAIN

My apartment looks out across the tranquil leafiness of St. John's Wood. High above the trees and the magnolia villas I can gaze down on a peaceful and pleasant scene. It is a prospect which never fails to soothe, whatever the season. But perhaps the moments I most enjoy are those few days in the year when the big picture windows are filled with snow and St. John's Wood is hidden behind a feathery white curtain. Then I stand before the glass staring raptly into the tumbling, whirling flakes. And instantly I am transported back down the years to a time of innocence, a time when a golden happiness sang in my heart.

❖ ❖ ❖

The year is 1935. I am six years old. I am squeezed up beside Papa in a horse-drawn sleigh. Behind us Mutti is telling Siche, my elder brother, to sit down and behave himself. Little Myer is asleep, his head in her lap. My big sister Paula, is snugly encased in her new navy coat and scarf and mittens and hat and ear muffs. All I can see of her is a red nose and an errant strand of blonde hair. Papa and I are sitting in the front seat beside the driver. The broad lapels of Papa's coat gleam with crystals as bright as diamonds. Ahead of us the horse clumps softly through the falling snow. I can hear the polished runners of the sleigh hiss as they cleave a path. There is a huge hooped frame over the horse's head and hanging from it are little silver bells which tinkle in time to every hoofbeat. I scrunch up my eyes and watch the wisps of snow eddy and dance in the hoop. There is a magic in the air.

On either side of the road huge fir trees stand like giants, their arms laden down with snow. I huddle closer to Papa, who puts his arm around me and says: "We'll soon be there, Susi."

But the track curves on forever through the silent forest. The pointed ears of our horse rise and bob as he draws us ever closer to Paradise.

And then we swing lazily round the last corner and there it is. Paradise. Or, as it is better known to its proprietor, the Hotel Esplanade. Siche is standing up again, but this time Mutti doesn't scold him. We are all leaning forward, peering through the snow at our fairyland castle. It is a huge alpine chalet, snug under a blanket of white. Beneath its brooding eaves, windows like bright eyes smile out at us, and even at this distance we can hear the muffled boom of the oompah band. I want to dance and sing and run in the snow and laugh all at the same time. Papa holds me tighter against his greatcoat. He too is enchanted.

Siche, of course, is first down off the sleigh. He peppers us with snowballs as we clamber down. Mutti's voice is sharp in the crisp air as she vainly tries to make him behave. We stamp our boots on the step and storm noisily into the hotel lobby, everyone talking at once. My mother brushes the traces of Siche's snowball off her black winter coat and she sighs, as if to ask God what she has done to deserve such a noisy, rebellious brood. But there is laughter in her eyes.

The proprietor of the Esplanade Hotel is a great big chunk of a man, as solid as the Tatra mountains which ring the valley. In his immaculate jacket and striped trousers, he is dignity personified. The dignity is quite wasted on us – for we prefer to call him Jumbo. Jumbo is a man of infinite patience and he needs every last atom of it whenever Siche comes to stay. The proprietor greets us as if we were his favourite nephews and nieces. He stoops to pat Myer's curls. Myer glares back ferociously. The proprietor tells Paula and me that we are the prettiest girls in his entire hotel. We giggle and blush. He turns to Siche who looks very smart and grown-up in his Tyrolean jacket with its gleaming brass buttons. "And what a fine lad you are," says the proprietor, evidently forgetting how on his last visit Siche gave half the staff nervous breakdowns by hiding in the luggage trunks and popping out like a jack-in-the box. Siche smiles the smile of a true innocent. But I know he is already plotting another prank to test Jumbo's mountainous patience.

Somehow Mutti manages to round us all up and lead us into the dining room, but no sooner are we through the door than we are off again to the four corners of the room. There are dozens of tables and at every one of them there are friends, some we haven't seen since this time last year. The meal is punctuated with whoops and shrieks. Every time I sit down I spy another special friend and I dart out of my seat to hug her. On the smoked pine walls gas mantles glow down like candles on the bloom-bright faces of a hundred laughing children. It feels as if we are at the biggest party in the world. And it is a party occasion. All of us here are Jewish. All of us are here to celebrate Passover. The mothers and fathers are also celebrating the freedom to be Jewish and to be together without fear. Up here in the mountains of Sudetenland they can forget Berlin and the dark shadows that grow longer every day. We children know nothing of the darkness. We sing and play as if this wonderful world will go on forever.

In the morning we can hardly eat breakfast because of the excitement in store for us. But Mutti and Papa hold us all in check long enough to polish off the crispy rolls and smetana and muffins dotted with mountain blueberries. We dash out into the snow, shouting with a sheer *joie de vivre* and catching the flakes in our mouths. Paula and I are dressed identically in what we would now describe as navy blue track suits with white edging. We strap our stout black boots onto snow shoes for the long walk up the mountain, for these are the days before T-bars and chair lifts. The distant summit of Schneekoppe, a great ice cream mountain, looms before us. Papa and Siche are each towing a toboggan. The climb takes us three hours. We could manage it faster but the moutainside is dotted with *Milchhauser* – little wooden booths – and we absolutely insist on stopping at every single one of them for hot chocolate and cakes.

Finally we reach the top of Schneekoppe. Spread out very far below our feet is the village of Spindlermuhle, looking like a sprinkling of doll's houses in the distant valley. On the mountain summit are *Bauden*, large single-storey huts, built like chalets. Inside each there is one enormous room, filled with our friends of the night before. The mothers and fathers sip *Gluhwein* while we cram ourselves with rice pudding. Half of the people here are from Germany, the rest from the Sudetenland and Czechoslovakian villages. They are not all Jewish but there is a warm companionable spirit. Around the wooden tables families gather to sing the lilting songs of the mountains. Papa snatches Mutti's hand and whirls her away to join the throng of dancers.

At last we have all had our fill of such merrymaking and we are ready for the day's great adventure – a helter skelter toboggan ride down through the pines to our beloved Hotel Esplanade. I sit shrieking on the front of one toboggan, Myer behind me, clutching my waist, and Papa behind him, holding the steering ropes. Papa is not the greatest navigator and our descent is a series of madcap dashes, each of them ending in noisy crashes into trees. The other toboggan, steered by Siche, is even more accident-prone, but this owes more to his wilful recklessness than mere mishap.

We end up outside the hotel in a couple of sprawling heaps, with everyone laughing and their cheeks aglow. The Esplanade is gleaming in the afternoon light. Already the gas mantles are lit and the jolly music of a Klezmer band spills out across the valley. We pull off our snow shoes and race each other into the lobby.

This is the time of the evening when all good children are supposed to go to their rooms and play draughts or board games, preferably without making too much noise. Sadly for our poor mother, we are not good children. And so instead we get down to the serious business of making mischief. Siche is clearly a master of the art, but his brother and sisters are eager apprentices. We help him amass a bunch of holiday postcards and watch giggling while he spreads black boot polish on the back of them. We charge after him down the stairs into the lobby where he takes up position and waits for his first victim. Before long, a guest comes through the double doors. Siche steps briskly forward and says: "Would you like to buy a postcard, sir?"

The unwary guest examines the pretty mountain scene which Siche profers to him. More out of kindness than anything else, the guest reaches in his pocket for a few pfennigs. In exchange he receives the postcard. He goes on his way. Only later, perhaps when he gets to his room, does he start to wonder why his fingers are stained with black polish. Then he will turn over the card and let loose an angry bellow about that accursed boy.

Inevitably, news of this latest prank gets back to Mutti and she gives Siche a severe scolding. "You are the naughtiest boy in the whole world," she says.

Siche looks penitent and promises to be good. But that night, while the hotel sleeps, he glides like a ghost through the empty corridors, collecting shoes from outside every door and redistributing them according to his own anarchic plan. In the morning it will take hours to untangle the chaos of his passing.

Mutti was right. Siche *was* the naughtiest boy in the whole world, and for that we are forever grateful. It was entirely thanks to his misdeeds that we survived the coming storm.

We often feared that the Hotel Esplanade would refuse to let us back because of his tricks. Yet somehow the proprietor forgave him and greeted us each time like his favourite guests. We went twice a year in '35, '36, '37, even '38. But the darkness that now engulfed all of Germany was slowly spreading to our mountain haven.

We noticed it first in the *Bauden*, where grim-faced men in brown shirts began to replace the friendly villagers. These men sat in their own half of the vast room. They did not speak to us or join in the festive songs. There was no open intimidation or harassment, so familiar now in the streets of Berlin. But the presence of the men in the brown shirts was a chilling reminder that even Paradise was tainted.

I remember vividly that last farewell, in April 1938. I was only eight but even children were aware that things were changing. In the restaurants, on the mountainside, the only talk was of how to flee the lengthening shadow of the Nazis. Some spoke of escape to America or England. Many dreamed of the Promised Land, a new life in Palestine. I can clearly remember two men discussing it earnestly at the restaurant table. One said: "Na also, wo ist denn, das Palastina?"

"Where is this Palestine?"

People were prepared to go to the ends of the earth, to lands they had only dreamed of. Anywhere to escape.

That last night all of the guests left more or less at the same time. Everything was as it always was. Outside in the snow, steam rose over the flanks of the sleigh horses, waiting in a long queue to ferry us to the railway station. Above the babble of voices I could hear the jangle of the sleigh bells just as I'd heard them so many times.

But this time it was so different. Every adult was weeping. Even the older children knew we were saying goodbye, not farewell. Mutti ran from friend to friend, hugging each one of them so dearly. The men prayed that we would all come together again, yet even as they spoke they knew it could never be. I saw through my tears the faces of my beloved friends. Yes, we will see each other soon, we promised each other.

I never saw them again.

The eyes of a poet, the mind of a great scholar – my paternal grandfather,
Reuben Joseph Neuwirth.

AN ACCIDENT OF BIRTH

Chance. Such a part it plays in the scheme of things. It was by chance, not design, that Papa was born in Czechoslovakia. His mother and father had a grand plan to uproot their young family and forge a better life in Poland. But then Papa came along and the grand plan was delayed. Papa was born on the third of January 1898. Markus Neuwirth entered the world as a Czech citizen. And the simple chance of where he was born means that I am alive to tell this story.

His first home was in the village of Satoraljaujhely – an impossibly long name for such a tiny hamlet – tucked away in the folds of the hills where they rolled down to the Hungarian border. There were already a few elder brothers and sisters in the cramped house. My Oma – grandmother – Rachel, was a woman of infinite resources. She was the sole breadwinner in the household. She also cooked, cleaned, fed the donkey, gathered firewood, nursed the children, and did everything else expected of a good mother. Not that Opa, my grandfather, a Hungarian by birth, was an idle man – far from it. Reuben Joseph Neuwirth was a natural-born scholar with his head forever buried in books. In Jewish families of that period this was not unusual. Oma believed, quite correctly, that the time her husband spent poring over books was an investment: that sooner or later his learning would free them from their humble existence. She *insisted* he devote himself to his studies and she looked after everything without complaint.

Opa was studying to become a *Dayan* – a rabbinical judge, settling disputes between Jewish neighbours. Month after month he sat by the table in his dark little house, a candle at his elbow and a stack of leather-bound volumes before him. To feed their rapidly growing family, my grandmother became a businesswoman. Every week she went to the wholesalers and bought stocks of cotton shirts and dresses. Then armed with her wares, she set off for the marketplace in the donkey-drawn cart. But making a living never came easy. The children, as soon as they were old enough, jumped on the laden cart and enthusiastically joined in the family business. The cart was not built for such a load and it often threatened to spill Oma, the children and her precious cotton bales into the muddy ditches. My Papa's earliest recollections were of the noisy marketplace, filled with bleating goats, squealing pigs, clucking hens, the cries of travelling vendors, the music of the gypsies, the clashing of hooves on the cobblestones and the hubbub of a hundred voices all talking at once. Papa loved every minute of it. In that raucous marketplace a salesman was born.

Meanwhile, Opa Reuben Joseph, without the children to distract him, was free to study the Talmud and centuries of law. He was a tall handsome man with a high clear forehead and the eyes of a poet. He had a long, straggly beard and he combed his fingers through it as he read the words of scholars long since dead. As my grandmother always knew, his long years of study would one day bear fruit. He rose to become a highly respected Rabbi, and then an appeal court judge in Berlin, a truly remarkable achievement for a Jew in 1930's Germany.

When Papa was only a few years old, the entire family upped sticks and made their delayed exodus to Poland. Home there was a *shtetl* in the foothills of the Carpathians. To call this *shtetl* a village would be to call a field a prairie. It was merely a handful of ramshackle houses on the outskirts of the southern Polish village of Kochin. Life there was every bit as precarious as it had been in Czechoslovakia. Oma added a new talent to her many skills – making oil for the lamps from *naft*, a crude kerosene.

The family home had a large room which served as kitchen, parlour and communal bedroom. In the centre of it was an enormous *Kacheloven*, a tiled oven where Oma baked bread and cooked by day. The fire in its belly never went out. When night fell, the children pulled out the benches on which they slept and formed them in circles around the mighty stove, with the youngest children having the warmest places. Winters in southern Poland are long and unforgiving so the *Kacheloven* was a basic necessity of life.

Opa returned to his books and Oma uncomplainingly resumed her role as provider. Her main stock in trade was gaily coloured dirndl skirts, kerchiefs, sheets, shirts and work aprons. There was table linen too for the better off customers at the weekly market in Krosno. Opa had chosen to settle near Kochin because of its closeness to Krosno, where there was a much greater market for Oma's wares. So, quite naturally, he expected business to flourish. After all, his wife was energetic, she was enthusiastic and she had a lively sales pitch. What could go wrong?

Opa had overlooked one minor detail: his dear wife was not exactly a shrewd businesswoman. She often became confused in the hectic haggling of the marketplace and didn't count her kopecks as wisely as she should. Before long, Opa began to notice something was wrong with the state of affairs. To be sure, Oma Rachel was doing a roaring trade, selling everything she ferried to market. But sometimes when they came to add up the day's takings, they found she had sold her cottons for less than they had cost her wholesale. Opa sighed deep into his beard. There was nothing else for it. He sadly closed his books and took over the running of the great family enterprise. Under his firm hand, the business began to show a profit for a change.

Papa took after his father in that he was tall and serious-minded. Like his brothers and sisters, he went to the *Cheder*, the Jewish school until he was eight years old. There they were taught by the Rabbi and they studied only Jewish subjects. Papa was already determined to be a businessman and he knew he needed a broader education, but there was not enough money at home to pay for it. So Papa saved enough kopecks from running errands and doing little jobs for neighbours to put himself through secular school. Every morning he prepared a crude sandwich of black bread and a hunk of cheese before walking miles along the muddied tracks to another village where he learned the rudiments of arithmetic and grammar. He was a ready pupil and in winter he daily braved blizzards and storms to attend school. His meagre store of kopecks allowed him to spend two years in its classes. That was the only formal education he ever had.

Grandfather's tremendous intellect was a legacy shared by several other members of the family. Of his first grandchildren, one went on to become the architect of Israel's present-day tax laws. Another, who sadly did not get out of Poland before the Nazis invaded, was a professor of mathematics at Warsaw University. That simple statement does not do justice to an almost unbelievable feat. Poland was riddled with anti-Semitism and Jews were disbarred from holding positions of prominence. For a man like my cousin to become a professor at the country's greatest university was utterly unheard of. It was a tribute to his genius and to the family's love of learning.

In my grandparents' *shtetl* life was still hard, but slowly it had begun to improve. Opa had realised his long-cherished ambition to become a *Dayan*. The local community was Orthodox and rather than have a civil court adjudicate on their differences, they preferred to have their legal rulings made by the *Beth Din*, the Judaic court. Opa Reuben Joseph sat in judgement on their cases and he was renowned for his great knowledge and benevolence. It was the first step in a distinguished career.

Papa was now a teenager, and an adventurous one at that. When he was just 14 he ventured south across the border into Czechoslovakia where he secured his precious citizenship papers. No one knew which way the world was turning, but it seemed a wise precaution.

Not that his Czech nationality did him any good when in 1914 the Great War rolled across the plains of Poland. The area where the family lived was under a repressive German regime. The north was the fiefdom of an equally harsh Russian administration. The people of Poland were caught in the middle. Orthodox Jewish families did their utmost to stay aloof from the hostilities – it mattered not to them who won, for the Russians were every bit as anti-Semitic. And so Papa, a strong and clear-eyed young man, concerned himself with trying to keep his business intact while War ravaged the countryside. But he did not count on the *dhapt* squads.

The squads were in effect press gangs. They roamed the country, snatching youths to conscript into the German-run army. In the

north, the Russians were rounding up peasants and similarly
reluctant Jews to serve as cannon fodder.

Papa was caught by the *dhapt* squad one evening as he returned
from Krosno. Their methods were none too gentle and he was led
away bloodied and bruised from his home. Within days he was in
the green uniform of the Polish army, a rifle on his shoulder. The
training was brutal and hopelessly inadequate. The barracks were
makeshift huts, infested with rats and fleas. The conscripts slept in
triple-decker bunks. Only weeks after he had been snatched from
the *shtetl*, Papa and a string of raw recruits were marched off to the
front. Without proper winter clothing, with only a meagre ration of

*Papa in October 1916, press-ganged into fighting – and almost dying for the
Kaiser. He is third from left on the top row, among other unwilling conscripts
in their primitive Polish barracks.*

food and barely able to handle his rifle, he found himself facing the Russian guns.

The conditions mirrored those in Flanders, except the rookies also had to contend with the bleak Polish winter. Those who survived the bombardment faced a slower death from starvation, disease or the cold. My father counted himself a very fortunate young man indeed: he was merely wounded.

At first his leg injury seemed too severe to treat at a crude field hospital, especially as gangrene and frostbite were rife in those primitive conditions. He was borne on a stretcher to a troop train, laden with hundreds of other wounded conscripts. Their destination was a military hospital in Berlin.

The War was over for Papa. but in the hospital he still faced a grim battle to survive. His bed was the floor and only the privileged had blankets. Food on the wards consisted of a thin vegetable broth and stale crusts of bread. There was not enough for the regular soldiers, even less for a reluctant conscript like Papa who had had to be beaten and forced into arms. But using his wits and his business acumen, he somehow managed to survive. He carried with him a secret cache of money. It was scarcely sufficient for his needs, but he spent his precious hoard buying cigarettes and selling them for a pfennig or two profit. That gave him enough to buy food from the black marketeers. He could even afford the wonderful luxury of a dirty army blanket. Slowly he began to regain his strength and he was able to take his first faltering steps. He was determined that he would not be left crippled, as was the fate of so many of his comrades. In his letters home he never once complained of the conditions or the pain. Within months he was walking normally. He did not even have a limp to show for his wound. He was able to walk from the hospital in the dying days of the War. He had beaten the odds single-handedly.

But the War claimed another casualty. Oma Rachel fell victim to typhoid which was devastating the war-torn villages. She died while Papa was still in hospital.

Her loss affected him dreadfully. It played a major part in his sudden decision to stay in Germany. He also felt Berlin offered a greater scope for his business and, ironic as it seems, Germany at that time was more tolerant of Jews than Poland.

Papa's first enterprise was conducted out of a suitcase. At lunchtimes he would do the rounds of offices, selling shirts, ties and whatever was the fashion of the day. He took a particular pride in his own appearance, always looking far more like a society gentleman than a humble salesman. He forswore the black garb favoured by other young men from Orthodox backgrounds and chose natty suits. He was especially proud of his dove grey spats. That was one fashion accessory he always loved, and even when he was an elderly man he still dressed in dark suits with immaculate spats resting on his polished shoes. His excuse was that he wore them for warmth. But we knew it was more for style.

In Berlin, Papa's business was going better than he had even dreamed. He found himself a flat in a house on the Oranienburger Strasse which had a thriving Jewish community. In the space of just a few years he transformed himself into a smart young man-about-town, well-versed in Berlin's rich cultural life. A promising future stretched before him. Now he felt was the time to bring the rest of his family out of the *shtetl*. This meant that Papa would be the breadwinner for all of them.

The elder brothers and sisters who were now married elected to stay in Poland. Opa and the others joined Papa in Berlin in 1921.

They shared a small flat in the Blumen Strasse, and it must have been a rather crowded one. Besides Papa and Opa, there were his eldest sister, Bertha, who took on the role of mother to the seven-year-old twins, Max and Betty. Papa's role was almost that of head of the family. He found a husband for Bertha and, of course, he provided her with a suitable dowry. He made sure the twins were properly educated. This paid handsome dividends, for Max eventually became the chief purser of the Israeli shipping line, Zim. The way Papa saw things, he was responsible for maintaining everyone: it was his natural duty. In due course he chose a husband for Betty.

There was just one thing missing from his life. Friends and relatives were beginning to ask: "Why has Markus not found himself a wife?"

But that was something he could not do. As was the way in Orthodox families his father must seek a wife for him. The importance of a father's position determined the choice of bride: she had to be from a matching background. As Opa was by now a renowned Rabbi, Papa's wife must also have a father of high esteem in the community. Therefore the choice was narrow. But among Opa's acquaintances was a man who was head of the Beth Din in Europe. Moshe Rothenberg was the greatest authority, the last appeal, in Rabbinical law. His position could be likened to that of the House of Lords in British law. His word could not be challenged. Moshe Rothenberg had a daughter, Mali, who was just a year younger than Papa. Opa and his friend agreed to introduce Markus to Mali through a *shadchan* – a matchmaker.

At first glance they were an unlikely couple. She had grown up in Germany, cocooned in privilege. She'd been to the best schools and had an abiding love of all the arts. She was a stranger to poverty and hunger. Unlike Papa's, her skin had never been cracked by the searing Polish winter. But I must not give the impression that the Rothenberg family lived in unconstrained luxury. Their home on the Blumen Strasse was a large apartment but it did not display the opulence one might associate with a man of his renown, nor was this the smartest address in Berlin. But Moshe Rothenberg chose to dwell among the community he served. Every morning there was a steady stream of callers to the apartment, each man seeking his intercession in one dispute or another. Moshe gave his time selflessly, for that was what his calling demanded.

Such was his fame, that I recall many years later on my first visit to Israel, I was attending a dinner when an accountant came up to me and asked in awe, "Is it true that you are Moshe Rothenberg's granddaughter?" I replied that I was and he said: "Well, I would like to shake your hand."

Mali was the second youngest of his six children. She took after her mother, Rachel, inheriting her petite stature and fair complexion. Even as a young girl she was very alert to the latest fashions. Somehow she contrived to be dressed *a la mode* yet in a way which was still decorous for the daughter of a very Orthodox family. She was well read and loved the opera. Her home was filled with music.

Mali trained as a secretary, mastering the intricacies and stylistic flourishes of High German. She had a wide circle of friends among the top echelons of Berlin's Jewish society. She was undoubtedly one of the brightest of the bright young things of her day. This then was the bride chosen for the boy from the *shtetl*.

The couple's cultural roots were identical, but their early upbringing could hardly have been more different. There was too a great physical disparity between them. Papa was tall, slender and very dark. Mutti, on the other hand, was small and plump, with blonde hair and serene blue eyes.

The way they were: despite their disparate backgrounds, Papa and Mutti were two perfectly interlocking pieces of a lifelong love.

Yet somehow the two hit it off from the moment they met. Papa took her to coffee houses, to concerts and to the early movie theatres. Their courtship was conducted with classic decorum and there was always a brother or sister in attendance.

Despite the difference in their origins there was an immediate rapport between Mutti and Papa. She loved his vitality and humour. He cherished her warmth and her quick intelligence. The two respective fathers sat back and congratulated themselves on their matchmaking.

And so Mutti and Papa married in Berlin in 1922. He was 24, and she 23. Life was good. They set up home and planned a rosy future. It was time to start a family.

STORIES FROM THE SHTETL

Siche was the first. He was born on the 31st of July, 1925. Paula arrived almost two years later, on the 31st of May, 1927. I came along two and a half years after that, on the 23rd of December, 1929. Myer's arrival on the 12th of October, 1931 completed our family.

When I was only one year old, the family moved from the Oranienburger Strasse to a magnificent apartment near the Tiergarten. I call it an apartment but it was as big as a spacious house. It was on the second floor of what was essentially a block of mansion flats.

Our front door opened onto a long wide corridor. Paula and I shared the first room on the left. It was our bedroom and playroom and, when we started school, our workroom. Myer had the room next door, and beyond that there was a huge airy lounge, one half of which was given over to a dining room, festooned with a diamond bright chandelier and with floor-to-ceiling doors opening onto the terrace. Beyond the windows rich clumps of red geraniums bloomed. At the end of the corridor on the left hand side was my favourite room of all, the *Herrenzimmer*. This served as Papa's library, study and refuge. Its walls were wood-panelled and it had an air of tranquility. It seemed to be imbued with Papa's own gentle nature. Outside the double-doors of the *Herrenzimmer* we children ran around the apartment making more noise than seemed humanly possible but here, within Papa's room, there was always a warm calm. I was supposed to do my schoolwork in my room, but more often than not I slipped away to the *Herrenzimmer* and took up residence on the black leather sofa, my legs tucked up under me. It always seemed much more conducive to thought in there. Along its walls there were beautifully carved cupboards and bookcases. In the centre was a walnut desk, littered with photographs, a black hand-cranked telephone and the impedimenta of Papa's business.

A wide terrace looking out on Agricola Strasse stretched along the entire left hand side of the apartment. Sometimes it was splashed with sunshine, sometimes, I suppose, it was dappled with raindrops or crusted with snow. But I remember only those sunkissed afternoons when we chased each other along the terrace.

Another balcony ran down the right hand side, past Papa and Mutti's bedroom, Siche's room, the maid's quarters, the bathroom and the kitchen. This balcony looked down on the inner courtyard of the flats. All of the rooms had soaring, lofty ceilings, decorated with finely-detailed friezes. It was a home built for gracious living, not that we children ever paid much attention to that.

My earliest recollections are of bolting down my breakfast in the kitchen before hurriedly dressing myself to accompany Papa on his business rounds. Mutti and Papa were always impeccably dressed and I knew I had to look my best if I was to go out with him. Fortunately they insisted on making sure we were every bit as smartly clothed. They bought all our clothes in Czechoslovakia, for the quality there was far superior even to that in Berlin's best shops.

So I always had a wardrobe of nice dresses and navy blue sailor suits from which to choose.

Together Papa and I walked the most fashionable streets of Berlin, calling on his customers. Along the way Papa entertained me with stories of his youth. Often he bought me an ice cream as a treat, but simply being with him was treat enough. Papa, despite his air of seriousness, always delighted in the company of his children so he also enjoyed our excursions together. Though I was too young to understand it then, the presence of a child by his side also served a very practical purpose: it gave Papa a certain immunity from attack. Already, gangs of thugs loitered by street corners, waiting to ambush and beat up solitary Jews, or any passer-by who simply looked Jewish. But even these louts were loath to attack a man with a little girl holding his hand.

My outings with Papa came to an abrupt end in September 1936 when I was six and a half. It was time for me to go to school. Up until then I had been taught in my own room by a succession of *Kinderfraulein*, German nannies. According to tradition, I set off for my first day at school cradling an enormous *Tute* – a cone of gaily decorated paper inside which were sweets and chocolates of every imaginable variety. Every child in the class had a similar treasure trove. I don't recall much of that first morning at the Adas School, save for the feast of sweets.

It was a highly respected school with a proud record of educating Jewish children. I must have learned something in my years there, but again my abiding memories are of mouth-watering treats. There was a tuck shop opposite the school and it became our first stop of the day. A pfennig bought me a *Nubuk*, a diamond-shaped bar of chocolate-coated toffee, plus a bag of multi-coloured boiled sweets, shaped like little pillows, plus a *Negerkopf*, a chocolate covered marshmallow. Armed with our stores of goodies, my friends and I would then cluster together to sample each other's purchases. I had always bought hard sweets in the sound logic that these would last longer. But I could never resist the tiny candy-coated eggs filled with liquid sugar, each egg no bigger that the nail on my little finger. If one of my classmates had bought those, I would swap half of my precious pillows for half of her irrestible eggs.

School was over for the day by one o'clock. It was time to put away our books and go off to lunch with friends. There were often distractions along the way. The Adas School in the Sigmundshof was on the banks of the Spree. As we crossed the bridge over the busy river we found ourselves facing a dilemma: to our right, the avenue led homewards, to an afternoon of fun and games. To our left was the huge grassy expanse of the Wullenweber Wiese, Berlin's equivalent of Hampstead Heath. Often it was playing host to a travelling fair. My friends and I would then forget all about lunch, preferring to munch on great pink clouds of candy floss. And after that we'd spend the last of our pfennigs on the *Riesenrad*, the giant wheel, shrieking and screaming as it spun us high in the air.

Or, if there was not a fair in residence, there was often another distraction, every bit as spectacular. The Wullenweber Wiese was also the take-off point for the Zeppelins, the giant airships. My friends and I would sit on the grass and watch the elaborate preparations to get these monsters airborne. There were always two Zeppelins taking wing together. The larger one was for passengers. We could see them wave gaily from the little windows of the gondola suspended beneath the great white balloon of the airship. The second Zeppelin was the command ship, overseeing the take off. Whenever there was a launch, the Wullenweber Wiese was bathed in a carnival atmosphere. Hawkers meandered through the crowds, selling lemonade and sweets. Above the noise of the throng you could hardly hear the airships' engines as they built up to take off. We watched the gangs of muscular men as they undid the mooring ropes. At last the giant craft were free of their chains. They seemed to hang there for a moment, and then they swam off in a lazy circle, for all the world like an enormous mother goldfish, tailed by her obedient baby. A great cry of delight arose from the crowd and everybody clapped. We watched and watched until the two vanished over the horizon.

One golden spring afternoon in May, 1938, we took up position in the meadow to see the mighty Hindenburg, the biggest airship of its day. We were already *au fait* with its scale and its achievements. Inside its vast envelope there were 190 million litres of hydrogen. From nose to tail, it measured 245 metres. It had already made ten transatlantic crossings, carrying wealthy passengers on a non-stop 6,000 kilometre voyage from the heart of Berlin to the shores of America. The Hindenburg was the undoubted king of the Zeppelins, so on this May afternoon it received an especially rapturous send-off. It rose majestically into the clear air, as if it was borne aloft on the cheers of the throng, ducked its nose, and billowed away westward. We waved and waved until our arms flagged.

A few days later, on the 6th of May, the Hindenburg exploded in a fireball as it touched down at Lakehurst, New Jersey. Some 36 of its 92 passengers perished. The disaster placed a full stop on the international programme to build fleets of passenger-carrying airships.

❖ ❖ ❖

Because of our age differences, we four children each had separate groups of friends and it was rare to find all four of us at home together during the day. But sometimes it happened. I would come home and hear, before the door opened, the sound of Paula reluctantly practising her scales on the piano. When I stepped into the hallway I was in immediate danger of being run over, for Myer used the long corridor as a racetrack. His red Mercedes pedal car posed a constant threat to life and limb as he tore up and down the carpet bellowing : "Beep! Beep!" From elsewhere in the apartment came the sound of Mutti's raised voice – a sure sign that Siche was home.

But amidst this bedlam there was a rock. A very unlikely rock, but one who was always serene no matter how stormy the day. This was Bianca, our Jewish housekeeper. She was dark and small, thin and of indeterminate age and I never saw her dressed in anything other than black. Bianca, despite her slight build, was mistress of every situation. She could control all of us, even Siche, with just one lift of her eyebrows. Her word was absolute law and none of us ever dared question it. Our nannies came and went, but Bianca was always there. She stayed with us to the very day we fled Germany.

This is not to say that Mutti left the care of us to Bianca. Mutti had a marvellous talent for spotting trouble brewing and she had a genius for defusing the potentially explosive situations that were bound to pop up among four such dissimilar children. Mutti's skill was such that she managed to quell her mutinous brood without harsh words, without threats. Before we knew it, the flashpoint was over and we were all behaving nicely again. Even Siche, who was not just hyperactive, but naughty too, was persuaded to be good. A less sensitive mother might have tried to make us conform, as if we were all alike. But looking back I can see that her gentle ways and her tolerance allowed each of us to grow to become his or her own person. And she ensured that when Papa came back in the evening, he returned to a welcoming home, where all the cares of the day had been smoothed away, like creases under a hot iron. In this way Mutti made certain that Papa was not burdened down with our childish squabbles.

❖ ❖ ❖

There was another key member of our household: Schwalb. Though strictly speaking, Schwalb was not of the household. He was Papa's long-serving *Prokurist*, the company secretary. In the office the buck stopped with him. His duties, however, extended to looking after us on the many occasions when Papa was perhaps away in Czechoslavkia on business or otherwise caught up in affairs. Schwalb was in effect a surrogate father, a challenging role for a quiet, self-effacing bachelor.

Schwalb – we never knew his first name, we never called him *Herr* – showed the same calm competence in his domestic duties that he displayed in the office. I do not remember him ever being cross, ever raising his voice to us. Looking back, I think Schwalb indulged us enormously. We children were certainly very fond of him.

He was a slight, bespectacled man who favoured light-coloured suits. When, a few years ago, I saw Schindler's List, I gasped at Ben Kingsley's performance as the factory manager. For in demeanour and appearance – right down to the clothes – Kingsley looked just like our dear Schwalb. Kingsley's duties were similar too – he was Schindler's trusted lieutenant. Though his responsibilities never extended to looking after four spirited young children.

You could liken Schwalb to a Jim'll Fix It figure: whenever there was a problem, Schwalb was on hand to deal with it, whether it was an unpaid bill in the office, or a dental appointment for one of us, or some urgent errand Mutti required of him. His name appears on all our birth certificates for he registered the births. He also registered us each new term at school. He took us on outings when we were proving too much of a handful around the apartment. Every time any of us think of Schwalb, we smile with fond memories. It is like recalling a much-loved uncle.

There is a sadness too. Schwalb was a German Jew, and as such was unable to secure a passport to freedom. Like Bianca, he fell victim to the Holocaust. After the War, my father spent months scanning the sheets of names coming from the displaced persons' camps where the emaciated survivors were housed. But he never found Schwalb or Bianca.

Now that I was at school, I saw much less of Papa and I missed him sorely. Often he did not come home from his business until after we had gone to bed, but he always made a point of calling in to see each of us. Though he must have been desperately worried by the savage degradation of Jewish businessmen which was now commonplace in Berlin, he always hid his anxiety from us. We grew up feeling safe and secure despite the tempest outside. Sometimes when he popped in to kiss Paula and me goodnight, we would beg him for a story. But he would simply put his finger to his lips and say: "Wait until Friday."

Every Friday evening in our apartment was a special occasion. It was the one night of the week when we four children took our meal at the big oblong table in the dining room. Mutti would light the Shabbos candles and we would take our places, looking freshly scrubbed and perfectly angelic. Bianca would enter with the first course, an enormous steaming tureen of chicken soup with *lockshen*.

The Shabbos dinner was a curious affair. There would be prayers and traditional songs, intoned by everyone with the greatest solemnity. But between them there were passages of unconstrained hilarity as Papa told us his tales of the *shtetl*. He told the same stories many times over but we never tired of them and we frequently begged him to recount a particular favourite.

Papa had a natural flair for telling anecdotes. He never hurried them. He told them at their proper tempo, dwelling on particularly comic moments. And all the time we children listened with our mouths open and the glow of the candles lighting our eyes. Papa introduced us to a gallery of larger-than-life characters from the *shtetl*. There was Motka the *Ganef*, the thief, Mottel the shoemaker, Joseph the rich man, Sadie the chicken plucker, Moshe the town crier, Yankel the innkeeper, and so many colourful personalities. As Papa talked I traced my finger over the acanthus leaves carved on the rim of the walnut dining table. This border echoed in small scale the ornate top of the giant walnut dining cupboard.

One story that always held me in thrall was the tale of matchmaking in the *shtetl*. When a young woman had reached marriageable age, her father, Papa recounted, would do the rounds of the neighbouring hamlets to find a suitable partner. This was frequently accomplished without the prospective bride or groom even being aware of it.

Sooner or later her father would chance upon a likely candidate. When that was the case, he invited the young man's father to the *schenk*, the local inn, to discuss the matter over several glasses of schnapps.

"My boy Aaron is a fine, strong son," one proud father would say. "He is still at his studies, but one day he will be a great scholar."

The other father was equally enthusiastic about the merits of his daughter. "And my Zlata is both beautiful and dutiful. She will be a good wife and mother."

Presently the two men, perhaps a little less sober than they should be, would agree that the young man and woman were ideally matched.

Next came the question of what size her *nadan*, or dowry, would be, and the two *shadchans* – matchmakers – had to settle on the terms of the *kest* – the number of years the families must support the couple before Aaron could earn a keep. When everything was agreed, one father would unloop his belt from his trousers. The two men would each hold one end of the belt. This little ceremony, known as a *kinyan-kaf*, was a formal agreement. Both fathers were pledged to it.

And once the *kinyan-kaf* had been performed, the two happy matchmakers would seal their contract with several more glasses of schnapps. Much later, and considerably the worse for wear, Zlata's father would roll home and tell his startled daughter, "Mazel tov – you have become a *kalah*" (a bride).

"Whose bride?" she would demand.

Meanwhile elsewhere in the *shtetl*, an every bit as startled Aaron was asking: "Whose groom?"

If the match went ahead, and more often than not it did, the town crier would tour the *shtetls*, bellowing out who was buying the happy couple which wedding presents. This useful service meant there was no risk the bride and groom would end up with duplicated gifts.

Sometimes the marriage brokers found their wishes defied. Papa relished the apocryphal tale of the young man who suddenly learns a *kalah* has been found for him.

"But what is she like? Is she pretty?" he questions his father.

"Yes, yes. Take my word, she is clever and good and interesting," his father assures him.

"But I still want to see what she looks like," the groom protests.

Nothing his father says can dissuade him, so he goes off to have a look at this bride they have chosen for him. He returns in dismay and tells his father, "It's no good: she's ugly."

His father philosophically spreads his hands. "What can I say? Either you like Picasso or you don't like Picasso."

These, and a hundred stories like them, brought tears of laughter to the family dining table every Shabbos.

TRAINS, RAINS AND A BOWL OF CHERRIES

When we were very young we used to holiday with Mutti every summer at Marienbad. For some strange reason the grown-ups never referred to these long breaks as holidays. Marienbad was of course a celebrated spa resort, famed throughout Europe for its natural water springs. Therefore Mutti and her friends would talk about going "to take the waters."

Papa, like many of the menfolk, chose to summer in Karlsbad, where the mineral springs had quite different, but equally efficacious properties. So each July the family would pack up and decamp to the spa towns for six or seven weeks. As far as the adults were concerned, we were going for the sake of our health. But we knew we were going on holiday, so the whole enterprise was launched with shrieks and whoops of joy.

Marienbad was the fashionable place to be seen. All Mutti's friends rented apartments there too, so there were always plenty of children for us to play with. The whole region, it seemed to us, was just one huge adventure playground, with hillside meadows amid

Papa, on the right, takes the waters in Karlsbad in the summer of '38.
The wives and children were enjoying their last summer in Marienbad.

which there were dozens of little groves where we could picnic out of the sun. We children roamed the wide open acres of the verdant parkland which curled up the sides of the hills.

Occasionally we went exploring and it was on these rambles that we discovered an amazing thing. When we reached the hill that bounded our park, we found that on the other side there was another sprawling land of forests and meadows, just like ours. And beyond that was another, and another, and yet more. They stretched away into the blue infinity.

Everywhere one looked there were woodland paths designed for children, where carved jolly little gnomes pointed the way. The parks were dotted with bandstands so that there was always music in the air.

Our mornings we spent almost sedately, accompanying Mutti to the springs to taste the sharp metallic water of the spas. I still have the little cut glass cup that I used to fill with the crystal clear water. Suitably fortified we then embarked on a marathon lunch in the big timbered restaurant.

The food in Czechoslovakia was much cheaper and of a better quality than one could find in Berlin. The helpings were king-size, too much for even our ravenous appetites. Every family had a huge platter with their name on it, so that you could come back in the evening and polish off the food you did not finish at lunch. My favourite part of those meals was the dessert course where we were served fruits you never saw in Germany. I still remember the taste of the big ripe comice pears and the luscious yellow peaches. They were a far greater treat for us than a whole box of chocolates.

At the weekends, Papa and the other men would often forsake the pleasures of Karlsbad to be with their families. Each time we would greet him as if he had been away for months.

Perhaps Mutti and Papa were right about the summer break being a health tonic. At any rate we always returned to Berlin in September brown and bright-eyed and several inches taller than we were before our holiday.

When I was five and a half I learned the true value of these health spas. I had developed severe eczema in my joints. It was painful and maddeningly itchy at the same time. There was one known cure for my condition – a visit to the spa at Rabka in southern Poland where the waters and even the air were rich in iodine.

The whole family planned to spend the summer there and to visit our various Polish uncles, aunts and cousins. But at the last moment Paula fell ill with a middle ear infection. These days it is the sort of ailment which can be remedied with a few doses of antibiotics. But they were not available to us then. The infection was regarded very seriously because it often left the sufferer with a permanent deafness. So Paula, attended day and night by a nurse, had to stay behind, as did Mutti and poor Myer, who was heartbroken that he could not share the grand adventure.

He and Mutti came to the station to see Papa, Siche and me off. The train was a great, gleaming monster, hissing out clouds of steam. We passed the second and third class carriages with their rows of spartan wooden benches, until we came at last to our compartment with its squishy leather seats and pretty little lamps. It was a 400-mile journey to Cracow, quite a test of patience for Siche and me. As the express thundered through southern Poland, I stood at the window, gazing out on the hamlets and *shtetls* which were already so familiar to me through Papa's Friday night stories.

The treatment at Rabka was painless and pleasant. I simply drank the water and breathed the air. The rest of the time I ran around in the sunshine enjoying myself as if there was nothing the matter with me. Within days of our arrival at the spa, the livid red eczema had begun to fade. In three weeks the marks – and the eczema – were gone, never to return.

The doctors told me however that I would probably develop hay fever as I got older. I was too young even to know what hay fever was. But they were right. After adolescence, my every springtime was blighted with sneezes and snuffles.

Now that my eczema was cured, it was time to enjoy the rest of our holiday. Papa had planned a busy itinerary. From Cracow we took the train for Krosno, and we were able to see the marketplace which had been the launch pad for Papa's business enterprise. It was just as he had described it. I looked around in wonder, remembering another of Papa's Friday night stories. It was in this very marketplace that Oma, well-pleased with the business acumen of her son, had told him: "You will always do well, Motka. You will always know the right things to say, the right things to do." It was both a blessing and a prediction. Papa carried Oma's words with him all the days of his life. It is true to say that he lived by them. Whatever misfortunes, whatever changes came along, he was always able to pick himself up and start again. And he always did well.

From Krosno a pony and trap bore us through the rutted lanes to Kochin. The countryside was a tapestry of pretty little farms set among rolling hills where fat white cows grazed in tranquil pastures. It was an idyllic rural scene that alas one cannot find today.

I was overwhelmed with excitement. I felt as if I knew everyone within the little *shtetl* through Papa's stories. There was one street, or a laneway which served as a street, but it seemed to be bursting with life, whatever the time of day. I wandered along it, fascinated by the clanging and banging, the neighing and the braying from the blacksmith's busy shed. There was the warm aroma of fresh bread from the bakery next door, the clack-clack-clack of the shoemaker busy at his shoe last, the cries of the tailors and the ever-present laughter of children.

The houses, if they could be called such, were humble affairs made of logs, with steeply sloping roofs, and beside each was a *stahl*, a lean-to shed to house the animals in the winter. The sets for the movie Fiddler on the Roof might have been lifted intact from the *shtetl*. The food here was very different from the sumptious repasts of Marienbad: but how I loved those open-air lunches when we drank warm milk, straight from the cow, and ate thick wedges of crusty bread with creamy white cheese.

Papa's old home had fallen into disrepair and was no longer habitable, but we stayed in the *shtetl* with my uncle. We were feted by everyone. So many of Papa's old friends came to visit because they wanted to hear how well he had done for himself. There was a great difference in one sense between us and the people of the *shtetl*: Theirs was a simple rustic life and they were curious to see visitors from the sophisticated city of Berlin.

We had the same VIP treatment when we moved on to Jaslo, another *shtetl*, where Taubshe, Papa's eldest sister, was living. Her house was much superior to the humble cottages we had seen in Kochin for she had married the son of the rich man from a neighbouring village. If this sounds an unlikely alliance, it must be remembered that her father, Opa Reuben Joseph, was a renowned scholar, therefore it was a great honour for the rich man to have Taubshe marry his son. Some years later she and my uncle lost almost all their fortune when a fire devastated the forests they owned, for these were the days before insurance.

The role of the rich man in the *shtetl* was an important one for wealth has its responsibilities. It was his duty to the community to see that brides from impoverished backgrounds were provided with a dowry. He also was expected to help penniless scholars through their years of study and to come to the aid of his farmer neighbours who faced hunger and ruin if their crops failed.

It was in my aunt's house that I first saw the wondrous *Kacheloven*, an enormous green-tiled range. I came to be very glad of that *Kacheloven* for it was in Jaslo that the rains began. At first we thought it was just a summer storm that would soon pass. But the next morning the skies were leaden with clouds and the single street of the *shtetl* was a quagmire of mud.

Aunt Taubshe insisted we stay until the rain stopped. But the next week it was still pouring down, flooding the low meadows and seeping through the cracks of the houses. At night it was bitterly cold outside, but I was wonderfully snug in my little bed beside the *Kacheloven*. Day after day we woke up to the drumming of rain on the roof. It seemed as if the rains would wash us all away. And in truth this deluge – the worst that anyone could remember – had already swept away the rail links with Germany and caused widespread devastation across southern Poland.

Papa decided we had all had enough. So one morning he got us dressed and packed and summoned a little cart to take us back to Cracow. My aunt provided us with a magnificent hamper of food and swathed me in a thick travelling rug. We lurched off into the driving rain with our donkey making heavy going of it, for more often than not the narrow track was more like a muddy stream. Every now and then we stopped at a farm to take on board milk, bread and cheese.

The journey to Cracow took several days, but I think Siche and I were enjoying the novel experience too much to complain about the bumps and jolts of the cart. I remember the magical feeling of being lulled to sleep by its rhythm.

We stayed for a short time in Cracow, a delightful town with plenty of distractions to please a couple of lively children. There were still many relatives to see in Poland but throughout the country the rail system was at a standstill. Tracks and points had rusted up so badly that trains could not run on them. The international lines were also affected and it would be several weeks before the Berlin express could get through again.

But at least the rains had stopped. We took whatever transport was available – usually a horse and cart – and headed north to the village of Tarnow to visit an uncle who was a most unusual man for his day. He was living apart from his wife, a situation which was virtually unheard of in the Orthodox community. This uncle did not have any children, and that helps explain what happened next.

That first evening he gave me a massive bowl of Morello cherries which were so overripe that the sugar in them had begun to turn to alcohol. Of course a five-year-old child knows nothing of such things. I just knew that the cherries were absolutely delicious and I ate and ate them until I fell asleep. It took them two days to revive me from my slumbers, for, not to put too fine a point on it, I was very intoxicated indeed. I cannot recall now whether I woke up with a hangover. But I was astonished that I had lost two whole days of my life.

We travelled on north to Warsaw to see other relatives I had previously only heard about. One of my cousins was a particularly striking man. In Orthodox parlance, he had gone native, for he dressed in the fashions of the day and mixed with Warsaw's cafe society. In those days before the War, Warsaw outshone Paris in its sophistication, and my cousin and his chic wife were among its brightest luminaries. He was the celebrated Chaim Schild, a mathematics professor at the city's university.

I was disappointed that I could not meet two other remarkable cousins, Israel and Meyer, for they had both gone to live in Palestine. Today Israel Shilat is better known there as Mr. Beersheba. He became the 26th citizen of Beersheba, then just a dusty little settlement on the fringes of the Negev desert. Now it is a bustling city of well over 100,000 people and he was its deputy mayor, a position he held for 26 years. He fled to Beersheba after he was sprung from Acre jail by fellow members of the Stern Gang during the time of the British Mandate. It was the biggest and most daring jail break of the emergency.

My cousin Meyer Schild became equally well known for drafting the tax laws for the fledgling State of Israel.

The railway to Berlin was now running again and it was time to return. But before we left, we embarked on a shopping spree, buying Mutti long strings of dried chanterelle mushrooms, for food was now becoming scarce in Berlin. We also spent a long time choosing toys for Paula and Myer. There were spinning tops, wooden dolls, cars, toy soldiers, all manner of things. But the undoubted star of our collection was a popgun made of light wood with figures carved on the barrel. We bought one for Myer and one for Paula, and then, because we couldn't resist them, we asked Papa to buy popguns for Siche and me. Little did Papa realise as he handed over the requisite kopecks that he had just instilled in Siche a passion for guns, a passion that would have a dramatic effect on all of our lives.

And so at last we returned to Berlin, just in time for Rosh Hashanah, the Jewish New Year. Myer remembers so vividly our homecoming and the sack of toys we had for him. Most of all he remembers the popgun.

Berlin seemed just the same as it had been when we left it three months earlier. Very soon we were to learn that things had changed.

A TALE OF TWO CITIES

Berlin in those days was a place of stark contrasts. For many it was the cultural centre of Europe and it acted as a magnet to the world's most innovative artists, musicians, writers, designers, composers and philosophers. Berlin's mastery of the new medium of cinema was supreme. In its technological advances and the brilliance of its *avant garde* directors and actors, it was envied even by the moguls of Hollywood. They flocked to its studios to lure this fresh talent to America. Marlene Dietrich became an international star after the studio talent scouts spotted her in The Blue Angel. Germany's great director Fritz Lang was soon Hollywood-bound too. In 1933, when Hitler came to power, his Propaganda Minister, Joseph Goebbels, offered Lang the job of German film industry supremo. Lang turned down the offer and that same night he fled the country.

In art, Berlin had usurped Paris as the forcing ground for new ideas. The *Bauhaus*, that great hive of creative genius, was revolutionising the face of world architecture, design and art. Its ranks included the Russian Kandinsky, Picasso's friend, Max Jacob from France, the Swiss Paul Klee and a host of others who were to become internationally renowned.

Charlottenburg, an area of imposing homes built for a more gracious era, became Berlin's equivalent of *la rive gauche* in Paris. Here the newcomers rented rooms behind the grandiose facades of the towering houses. There was a truly bohemian air to the district. The sinister shift in German politics was not echoed here, and Jewish creativity was allowed to flourish. Thus playwright Kurt Weill, existentialist philosopher Martin Buber, composer Arnold Schoenberg and artist Max Liebermann all held their rightful prominence within this free-thinking society.

And somewhere in a rented room, the English author Christopher Isherwood was eking out a precarious living as a tutor. Between English lessons he also began work on the novels "Goodbye to Berlin" and "The Berlin Stories," which later formed the basis for his play "I Am A Camera," and later still would be source for the film "Cabaret," that most unflinching study of how the Weimar decadence led to Nazism.

Soon this artists' colony would be purged by the Nazis and its leaders would be forced to flee – Schoenberg to Paris, satirical cariacturist George Grosz to America, Kandinsky to France, composer Paul Hindemith to Switzerland, Brecht to Sweden. But in the early Thirties, the city was still a haven to all that was new and daring. It had glamour, it had style, it had culture.

That was the face Berlin presented to the world.

But away from the jostling coffee houses of the Charlottenburg, Berlin had a darker face which so many did not see until it was too late. It could be found in the *Bierkeller*, where jobless disaffected men gathered to bemoan their fate and seek a scapegoat.

I caught a glimpse of both faces. My mother's sister, Jenni Fluss, had married a very wealthy man and they lived in an imposing mansion block in the Charlottenburg, where every apartment had an entire floor to itself. We went to visit them often and I loved the sheer vibrant mood of the district with its babble of foreign tongues. The fine restaurants played host to a colourful cafe society of brilliant young men and women. It was a dazzling time.

Other parts of Berlin also managed to hold on to their character despite the canker of Nazism eating its way across the city. I had a dear schoolfriend, Irma, whose family used to invite me for picnics on the banks of the Wannsee. Here there was a bathing lido where the flower of Germany's aristocracy frolicked as if there was nothing to fear. In a few short years Wannsee would lose its innocence. It was here that the Nazis signed some of their most barbaric decrees.

Other times I would go with Irma to Grunewald, Berlin's answer to the Bois de Boulogne, and watch the young scions of the German nobility exercise their horses. It was too a favourite spot for the wealthy car owners who would parade their prized toys through the sunlit avenues of Grunewald. It was a place where the fashionable just had to be seen. This was my introduction to a cosmopolitan world, far brighter, more scintillating than anything I could imagine.

All of this was a source of wonder and enchantment to me. As our family was Orthodox we naturally led a more conservative lifestyle, and neither Grunewald nor the Wannsee featured in our social landscape. Irma's parents, although Jewish, felt themselves to be wholly assimilated into the German culture. Indeed, they sometimes saw themselves as more German than many Germans. Her father was a rich banker and very well connected, therefore he felt at home among the privileged classes of the society circuit.

He never for one moment suspected that the dark shadows emanating from the *Bierkeller* could ever threaten his peaceful world. After all, he was a German, first and foremost. Why should he be afraid? There were many who felt this way. Some had even fought for their country in the Great War and had medals for valour. How could they be deemed enemies of the people?

So many found out only too late that a Jew could not be a German in Hitler's brutal new order. Irma's family were branded unfriendly aliens and rounded up in the first wave of the Holocaust. My dear friend and her entire family perished in the concentration camps.

That came much later. Before then I had already seen the decadent side of our neighbours. Mutti employed a daily cleaner, a fat, jolly German woman who had no children of her own. She was fond of me, and – as I did not have to attend school in the afternoons – I would often go to her home, a sub-basement flat, for lemonade and cakes. Their small apartment, consisting of a bedroom and a living room, was stuffed with heavy dark furniture. The little window set high in the wall served only to make it look more gloomy. Yet at first I enjoyed going there. She and I went on shopping trips together and it was on these excursions that I picked up her Berlin patois, learning the working class dialect which is as much part of the city's voice as cockney is that of London's.

Her husband was a very fat and friendly man who in the beginning greeted me warmly. But the story of this couple is typical of the day. He, like tens of thousands of others across the city, lost his job and in the depths of a recession there was little hope of his finding another. He began spending his days hanging around the *Bierkeller*, which were becoming the Nazis' most fertile recruiting ground. Before long he had swallowed the propaganda that a Jewish-Bolshevik conspiracy was to blame for his plight. He joined the Party. Suddenly he belonged to a brotherhood. No longer was he a little man without a job, he was part of a powerful new movement.

His wife remained the kindly woman she had always been but I soon began to detect the change in him. It must have been a bitter pill for him to swallow that the only money coming into his household was his wife's earnings as the maid to a Jewish family. But she could not afford to stop working. She still invited me home with her.

Her husband began to change towards me. He openly spouted Nazi propaganda, citing the Jews as the cause of the nation's ills. After each little outburst he would say, "Of course, I don't mean you. I mean *other* Jews." His wife, for her part, always looked away in embarrassment.

In this way so many previously decent German people paved the way for genocide, without ever stopping to think that human beings might be concerned. They were always talking about *other* Jews.

On one occasion the couple took me to a *Biergarten*, where I first heard the rabble-rousing drinking songs. All around me were large men downing steins of beer and sharing a rough companionship. Many of them were already in the Party, most of the others would soon join. Their hatred of Jews was quite open. A lot of them were basically decent people who knew they were behaving badly but they could not help themselves. I sat quietly in the *Biergarten* and sipped my lemonade. We children already knew to be afraid, even if we did not know what to fear.

Presently I stopped going to the couple's apartment: it was no fun any more. I'm sure the husband was just as relieved that he no longer had a little Jewish girl despoiling his Aryan home.

I was already learning that one could not tell friend from foe. People who had worked amicably with Jews for years changed so rapidly. Overnight they became nasty and abusive. The porter in our flats who once greeted us with a smile now scowled and insulted us openly. Others, who had no truck with the Nazis, let us know in small secret ways that they did not share this blood hate. But their soft voices were soon drowned by the roars of the mob. We learned not to trust anyone, for we never knew who next would turn against us.

Now that my eczema was cured, I was able to throw myself body and soul into a new passion – gymnastics. I was tall for my age and quite lithe, and the demanding discipline of the exercise appealed to me. Of course we did sports in school, but I also took evening classes, practising for hours on the parallel bars and vaulting horses.

At one time I thought of little else but my next visit to the big airy gymnasium. It was my life. I found myself suddenly interested in all sorts of sport, even the spectator variety. This was in 1936 and there was one burning topic in Berlin conversation, the forthcoming Olympics which the city was to host. Even the grim spectre of Nazism was temporarily forgotten as Berliners fiercely debated who the new Olympians would be. Everyone had their own cast iron opinions and the arguments raged on day in, day out. Naturally, my main interest was in who would take the gold in gymnastics, but the whole spectacle of the games enthralled me. I was every bit as excited as any little German girl of my age.

These were times when Jews were already learning to keep a low profile if they wished to avoid trouble. That meant we had to be careful where we went, for under the Nuremburg Law of 1935, Jews were deprived of their rights as citizens.

But one fine summer's day I slipped out of the house and set off for the Tiergarten. I did not tell Mutti where I was going for, had she known, she would have forbidden it. I walked down to the Schoenhauser Allee which was not quite as simple as it sounds, for hundreds of thousands of Berliners were heading the same way.

When I eventually reached my destination, I found myself amid the biggest throng of people I have ever seen in my life. Either side of the broad thoroughfare was lined by crowds twenty or thirty deep. There was a tremendous hubbub of voices and above it all came the stirring notes of brass marching bands. This was the first – though highly unofficial – event of the long-awaited Olympic games. Everyone was feeling immensely proud and patriotic. They waited with patient good humour for the spectacle. I wasn't quite sure what we were waiting to see, but I was just as anxious to see it. Unfortunately, in front of me was a solid wall of stout Berliners and I couldn't see anything. It took me the best part of an hour to squeeze through their ranks until I found myself squashed up behind the crash barriers with a grandstand view of the event. I suppose my first reaction when I got to the front was one of disappointment for there was nothing to see. The majestic sweep of the Schoenhauser Allee was empty, but for the sight of a band disappearing into the distance. So I looked at my neighbours instead. It seemed as if every single one of Berlin's four million citizens was there, all of them smiling, all of them cheering. Many were brandishing German flags with the now familiar swastika. They were not proclaiming any particular loyalty to the Nazis, they were merely demonstrating their pride in Germany's role as Olympic hosts. Many others were waving Italian flags, though I could not understand why. The one thing I know is that I cheered as lustily as anyone in that huge mass. The mood was indescribable. We were one big happy family of Berliners celebrating the greatness of our city. There were frail old grandfathers leaning on their sticks and bewildered babes in arms, there were labourers in blue dungarees and dapper city gents, nurses in crisp white uniforms, old ladies in black shawls. But we were united in our elation and we sang and laughed and waited for whatever it was to arrive.

All along the carriageway was a skeletal line of crash barriers, and every few yards there was another SS man, resplendent in black with a blood red swastika arm band. Even these iron-faced men seemed caught up in the spirit of the moment for they were smiling. So too were the brownshirted Storm Troopers and the boys in the uniform of the Hitler Youth in the crowd beside me. For once there was nothing to fear.

Suddenly, a long way off came a deafening roar of cheers. I craned my neck to see why the crowd was cheering. All I could make out was the distant sight of a car coming towards us and travelling very slowly. As it got closer, so did the roar, and eventually I could make out what the people were shouting:

"Sieg HEIL! Sieg HEIL! Sieg HEIL!"

Around me my neighbours were holding aloft their little Italian and German flags and brandishing them furiously. The car crept closer.

And then it was in front of me. It was a large open top Mercedes tourer with swastikas mounted on the bonnet and on either wing. I had already recognised the two men standing stiffly in the rear of the car.

One was tall and plump as a capon, with a full moon smile. I knew him from the newspaper photographs. Here was *Il Duce*,

Benito Mussolini. I now understood the presence of the Italian flags.

His companion was of course Adolf Hitler. His face was in comic contrast to that of the Italian Fascist leader. Beneath the ridiculous moustache, his mouth was pursed grimly in a thin approximation of a smile. He was the only person in the entire length of the Schoenhauser Allee who was not beaming.

Mussolini was dressed in black, Hitler in brown. They had their arms upraised in the infamous Nazi salute. As one, every man and woman around me raised their flags in the same flat-handed gesture. I did not have a flag. I just cheered.

The Mercedes drew level. Adolf Hitler was only five or six yards away. He kept his washed out eyes focussed straight ahead, seemingly oblivious of the salutes and the tumult of voices. He was certainly oblivious of the little seven-year-old Jewish girl pressed up against the crash barrier, cheering his triumphal progress,

No doubt inside he was congratulating himself on having pulled off a superb propoganda coup by hijacking the Olympics for his own squalid political ends.

The effect of the crowd's collective mood was mesmerising. I cheered and cheered until my throat was raw. Behind his Mercedes came a huge cavalcade of the Party hierarchy – Himmler, Goebbels, Goering, Speer, Hess, Heydrich. They were all there. And still I cheered.

When at last this terrible carnival of monsters had finally passed, I slipped off home, well pleased with the day's spectacle.

As I said: we children already knew to be afraid, but we did not know what to fear.

A LIGHT IN THE DARKNESS

Around us the world was going insane, but we were too young and too cocooned by our parents to notice. Our childhood was in many ways no different from that of Jewish children in London or New York.

The centre of our universe then was the local cinema. It had a proper name of course but we referred to it only as the flea-pit. It was a place of secret trysts, where blushing young girls and awkward boys held hands in the flickering shadows. I had my first dates there, though I don't believe we ever got as far as holding hands. Mostly, the neighbourhood cinema was just a place where we could all meet up and gossip.

Every street corner had its own flea-pit. These were a far cry from the purpose-built movie theatres of today. Our favourite haunt was just a large room in a converted house, its walls painted matt black. The admission price was a single pfennig. But more often than not we slipped in for free. It was more fun that way.

The "lobby" of the flea-pit was merely a hall. The doorway to the cinema was screened off behind a great many layers of thick black sheets of material which kept out the light from the street. We used to wait until the ticket collector had gone off for a coffee or was perhaps engrossed in the film herself, and then, giggling, we would wend our way through the thicket of curtains.

Inside, to the right, was a piano, where a stern-faced woman banged out heavy chords to accompany the film. This was, after all, in the silent movie era. Beyond her were rows and rows of plain chairs, most of them already occupied by our friends. I don't imagine that the flea-pit made much of a profit, for often there were more gatecrashers than paying customers.

Once seated, we would get out our sweets and settle back to enjoy the film. I always treated myself to a *Nubuk* – a bar of chocolate-covered nougat – because I could manage to make that last all the way through.

The flea-pit had a highly varied bill of fare. One day a western, the next a Keystone Cops romp or a melodramatic romance. Every star had his or her fans and I had a soft spot for the dark, brooding good looks of Rudolph Valentino. But everyone's undisputed favourite was Charlie Chaplin. Those hard wooden chairs rocked to our laughter every time the flea-pit played one of his movies. If the flea-pit had had aisles, we would have been rolling in them.

All over Berlin, German children were laughing just as loudly at Charlie's antics. But soon the laughter would stop, for his films were banned by the Nazis: he was in part Jewish, therefore he could not be permitted to make Aryan children happy. Chaplin had the last laugh when, in 1940, he released his first talkie. *The Great Dictator* was a biting satire on the strutting, swaggering, self-important figure of Adolf Hitler. It earned Chaplin plaudits throughout the free world, and a starring role on Hitler's personal death list.

Our flea-pit was next to the bakery which played a vital role in the way we lived. In those days the typical apartment kitchen had gas rings, but no oven, therefore the bakery was an essential service to the community. Any time anyone had a dish which required oven cooking, they took it to the shop beside the cinema. I remember that each time we emerged from the flea-pit, blinking in the sunshine, there was the most fragrant smell imaginable emanating from busy ovens next door.

The staple fare was of course bread and cakes. Each Shabbos, every family in the neighbourhood sat down to *challa* bread provided by our local baker. He also supplied the various ceremonial breads used in the celebrations of our faith. When Myer was born, Mrs. Garten, a dear friend of Mutti's, prepared the plaited *challot* bread for his *brit*, the circumcision ceremony.

Mrs. Garten had a wonderful natural flair for cooking, a flair which was readily recognised among her neighbours. They often asked her to prepare special dishes which the baker would later pop into his ovens. She was, I imagine, a precursor of the private caterers one finds nowadays. I always regarded Mutti's friend as the best cook in the world. And on the occasion of Myer's *brit* she excelled herself, preparing the most impressive loaf I have ever seen. It was quite wide and at least a metre long, perhaps half that again. Indeed, it was so impressive that the baker asked Mutti and Mrs. Garten if he could display it in his shop window until it was needed for the ceremony because he had never baked such a beautiful bread. There it reposed for a few days, a tribute to Mrs. Garten's skills. And of course a powerful advertisement for the bakery.

The ovens were also much in demand for cooking *tcholent*, a thick nourishing stew which contained potatoes, barley, meat, whatever fresh vegetables were available, and no less than three different varieties of beans. But every family had its own recipe. Once the dish had been prepared in the kitchen, one of us bore it down to the bakery. *Tcholent* required slow cooking so that all the flavours were intermingled, and it simmered gently in the oven all through the night. When it was cooked, it was absolutely delicious. I still make *tcholent* three or four times a year – although now I no longer need the services of a baker – and each mouthful reminds me of those days in the Agricola Strasse.

The Nazis' campaign to intimidate and harass the Jews was rapidly escalating. Harassment took many forms. There were the street corner thugs who could maim or even murder passing Jews without fear of prosecution, for Jews had become non-persons. There was widespread vandalism, and the desecration of synagogues. There was the summary dismissal of all Jews in official positions.

And there were more subtle ways of reminding Jews that they were without rights. One of the more bizarre was the great black-out exercise of October 1938. Ostensibly this was an air raid drill, to determine whether Berlin was in readiness to defend itself in the event of an RAF bomber attack. But the timing of this drill was not lost on us. It took place on the night every Jewish family in Berlin sat down to enjoy the Rosh Hashanah dinner.

No one had black-out curtains and even the light of a single candle was forbidden. Outside in the street the SS checked every window for the faintest flicker of light. The glow of a candle would be sufficient excuse for them to hammer on the door and arrest Papa.

So we faced the unhappy prospect of celebrating the new year in complete darkness. Then Mutti had a brainwave.

"Myer," she said, "go and fetch your toy fire engine."

Myer was clearly puzzled by this strange request, but he did as he was told. Mutti took the fire engine from him and placed it in the centre of the table, where the candles normally stood. And finally we grasped Mutti's bright idea.

The fire engine, you see, had a little red light on its roof, powered by a battery. Mutti switched it on and a soft red glow spilled out across the table linen. It was a decidedly weak light – certainly not strong enough to be spotted by the watchers in the street below – but it was sufficiently bright for us to see each other, and, more importantly, the food.

We gathered around the table, dressed in our very best clothes. Mutti bowed her head over the little red light and solemnly recited the traditional prayer:

Blessed be Thou, O Lord our God, King of the Universe, who commandest us to light the Shabbos candles.

The feast began. The sense that we were defying Hitler gave an extra edge of celebration to our Rosh Hashanah meal. If anything, it was more enjoyable than ever, thanks to Mutti and Myer's little red fire engine.

The German State under the Nazis functioned like a machine, but often it was not a terribly efficient machine. This became clear in 1938 when Hitler launched a systematic purge to expel non-native Jews from Germany. The logical process would have been to seek

out all Jews with foreign passports simultaneously, but the Nazis
could not cope with this.

What they did instead was to target, for example, the Polish
Jews exclusively for a period. They would round up as many as they
could find, pack them into sealed trains and dump them over the
border in southern Poland. Then, when the Nazis were satisfied
that this particular piece of ethnic cleansing had been
accomplished, they would move on to the Czech Jews, or those
from Romania or Hungary. In the smaller towns they netted whole
families, but in Berlin they did not have the manpower to do that, so
they contented themselves with tracking down the husband,
confident that his family would be forced to follow him across the
frontier.

There was one fatal flaw in this system: when the State was
hunting down Polish Jews, they would simply hide in the homes of
neighbours who belonged to another group, not yet targeted. So I
became used to the sight of dozens of strange men suddenly using
our lounge as a dormitory until the purge on them was ended. On
one occasion I remember the lounge, the dining room and the
Herrenzimmer were all packed with fugitives. There must have been
well over a hundred strange guests sharing our apartment.

News of a fresh sweep went through the community like jungle
drums. As soon as one man was arrested, his family raised the
alarm, warning others to hide, or, as we called it, to go underground.

Many of the hunted men arrived in our home with pots of soup
or chicken or stew. Others had learned of the purge only at the last
minute and they turned up empty-handed and hungry.

Often my first chore in the morning was to run down to the
corner grocery store and order emergency supplies of bread, butter,

cheese and kosher salami. The grocery shop was also a clearing house for information which I picked up and relayed to Papa.

The whole community responded magnificently to these raids. The men on the run were warmly welcomed by their hosts and treated as members of the family. After all, the next week it might be the host's turn to seek a hiding place. When the Gestapo switched their attention to the Czech Jews, Papa found shelter with a Polish friend and he was safe there as, for the time being, they were not bothering the Polish community.

Naturally, when we had guests, they were anxious to let their families know they were safe and well. This was another job for me. I was often dispatched to go through the streets around the Tiergarten, passing on messages from husband to wife and vice versa. At the time it seemed like a great adventure.

The roundup usually lasted only a few days and then it was safe for the men to return to their families again, at least until the next dragnet.

The first sign that a raid was in progress was the sudden and very noisy arrival in the street outside of several cars and trucks, filled with police, the SS and, occasionally, the Gestapo.

This strike force would then clatter up the stairs of an apartment block, banging on every door. If any resident was not at home or was slow to answer the thunderous knocking, the police would simply batter down the door.

Meanwhile the entire block was cordoned off by armed men to prevent anyone fleeing. The guns were not merely for show.

Our apartment was the target for several raids. Whenever the SS banged on our door, Mutti would answer it. She had a wonderful sense of self possession. She would look up at these thugs, her face serene and composed, and ask: "Yes? Can I help you?"

The SS evidently had never gone to charm school. They would merely elbow her aside and begin combing the rooms. Inwardly Mutti's heart must have been racing but she was determined they would not see her fear. They would push her into the kitchen and subject her to a barrage of questions about where Papa was. Mutti would simply shake her head ruefully and say: "I'm sorry. I can't help you. I don't know where Herr Neuwirth is at present."

As she was being questioned, other officers were systematically searching every room. They rapped on wood panelling to see whether there was a secret compartment, they got down on their hands and knees to peer under the beds, they ransacked through our toy cupboards. Each bedroom had large walk-in closets for clothes and the searchers diligently ferreted through them. These raids might last an hour or more, after which the frustrated squad would pull out (they never apologised, they never said goodbye) and go off to terrorise another Jewish family.

Since as early as 1936 we children had been schooled by our parents never to reveal *anything* to the SS. Papa told us: "Whatever they ask you, you say you don't know. No matter how apparently innocent the question might be, you don't know."

Of course I never dreamed that I might be grilled by the Nazis. After all, what could they want with an eight-year-old girl?

And then one humdrum afternoon when I was sitting reading in the kitchen, we heard the now-familiar sound of trucks screeching to a halt in the Agricola Strasse. This time Papa was not in hiding – he was away on business. But the rule of silence still applied. As we waited for the knock on the door, Mutti turned to Paula and me and said: "Now remember, don't tell them anything."

The raid followed its usual course. A torrent of questions directed at Mutti and the sound of heavy boots clacking on the wooden floors. Paula and I sat in the kitchen, trying to make our faces as expressionless as possible. They would soon go away, we thought.

But not this time. The senior officer, angered and frustrated by Mutti's unhelpfulness, looked around for someone who might be more forthcoming. His eye fell on me. He grabbed me by the arm. "Come!" he commanded.

For once Mutti's calm demeanour was shaken and Paula's face was ghostly pale. I heard Mutti protesting as I was tugged along the corridor into my bedroom, with a second SS officer hard on my heels. This second man pushed Mutti back and closed the door behind us, then with studied deliberation, he turned the key in the lock. I could never understand why. Where did they expect a little girl to run to?

Neither man smiled. I backed away across the room until I felt behind me the huge table at which Paula and I did our homework. The bedroom was a bright airy place with cream-coloured walls and wide French windows opening onto the terrace. I always loved that room because of its sense of space. But at this very moment it seemed as dark, as cheerless as a grim prison cell.

My fingers clenched the rim of the table and I looked fearfully at my interrogators. Their very appearance was calculated to instill fear. They were both tall men, dressed in the dreaded black uniforms of the SS. Their black leather boots were polished to a high shine, as were the buttoned pistol holsters on their belts.

I looked beyond them and saw against the far wall Paula's bed and my own, each sprinkled with an assortment of dolls and toys. In one corner was my blue scooter. The two men closed in so that now each was standing only a few feet from me on either side. I suddenly felt very small, very alone and very afraid.

One officer began the interrogation with a sharp-edged question.

"Where is your father?"

"I don't know."

His colleague asked: "When did you last see him?"

I looked at the SS insignia on his collar and I was half-paralysed with terror. After a moment I stammered: "I can't remember."

They laughed, but there was no humour in their laughter. I stood there, still in my school uniform of navy blue skirt and white blouse. I did not know whether they were going to hit me or shoot me. I could feel the blood pulsing in my head and my legs were trembling. I felt they would give way under me at any moment.

The SS tried again. "You must know where he is. Is he in Berlin?"

I shook my head. "I do not know."

I knew exactly where Papa was. He was across the border in Czechoslovakia, ordering a new consignment of textiles. Perhaps if I had told them that they would have left me and gone elsewhere. But then they might have alerted the border guards to arrest Papa as he tried to return.

But I think what was paramount in my mind was Papa's oft-repeated instruction: "Never tell them anything."

And I remembered Mutti's quiet composure. I became equally determined that these two hulking brutes would not have the pleasure of seeing my terror. I took a deep breath and stood upright.

One SS man stared at me intently. "Who are your father's friends?"

I shrugged. "I don't know."

"But you must know," his partner shouted. "Who comes here? Who does he visit? Where do they live?"

The questions went on and on. I refused to waver. If they had given me a mark for every time I said "I don't know," I would have been the richest little girl in Berlin.

They threatened and shouted, to no avail. They tried a different tack, smiling and making their voices soft and cajoling. But those smiles were as friendly as a crocodile's. I stood rigidly to attention with Papa's warning echoing through my brain: *Tell them nothing.*

The SS were not like the street corner Nazis. They were the intelligentsia of the police state. These two tall men in my bedroom were fully-trained interrogators, schooled in the art of terror. An aura of menace clung to them. They knew it and they were proud of it.

The grilling went on and on and on. I must have been locked in there for a couple of hours, all the time insisting I knew nothing of Papa's whereabouts.

In the end, they turned away in disgust and gave up. I heard them march off down the corridor. I stayed in exactly the same position until I heard the slam of the front door, signalling that the search squad had left.

Only then did I allow my pent-up tears to flow. I ran shrieking for the comfort of Mutti's arms. She hugged me to her breast as I sobbed out those two hours of terror. I cried until I had no tears left to shed.

But later there was a strange elation. Once again we had outwitted the SS. Once again Papa had evaded the hunters. For us, there was a tremendous satisfaction in cocking a snook at Hitler in this way. It was almost like a game. And then something happened which changed everything.

One November morning in 1938, just before six o'clock, I was up and preparing for school when the back doorbell rang. Mutti was still in her bedroom and did not hear the bell. Bianca was otherwise engaged, so I went to see who our early bird caller might be.

I opened the door and there before me stood our milkman. It was most unusual for him to come to the door in this fashion. Usually he simply left the milk and went on his way, clanking bottles at every step. He was a roly-poly man, dressed in a dark blue uniform, with a matching *Schildkappe*, a little round peaked cap, perched on his head. Normally his dark button eyes crinkled into a smile whenever he saw us. But this morning they were grim and unsmiling.

He said: "I must speak with your mother."

Naturally, I was curious and I asked him what it was about. He simply repeated: "I must speak with your mother."

I ran to Mutti's bedroom and told her. She was equally mystified about why the milkman should demand to see her. After all, these small domestic duties were always seen to by Bianca. But Mutti put on her dressing gown and went to see what this was all about. I tripped along behind her, my curiosity whetted.

The milkman's first words to her were sombre. He said: "Under no circumstances let the children go to school today."

If anything, this only deepened our perplexity. Mutti asked why.

He said: "Because there has been a lot of trouble through the night. Don't – whatever happens – let them go to school. It is not safe for any of you to go out."

Mutti was not the sort of woman who let others dictate what her children should or should not do. She tossed her head and began to argue with him. But the milkman was absolutely insistent and his earnest tones made her realise it would be wise to follow his advice.

She asked him what sort of trouble there had been, but he did not have the details. All he knew was that Jews and Jewish businesses had been attacked during a night of organised violence.

Mutti at last understood that the milkman was acting out of kindness and concern for our welfare. She thanked him and he slipped off to warn other Jewish families. Oh yes, there were still many righteous Gentiles in Berlin.

That early morning call came on the 10th of November, 1938. It was our first inkling of *Kristallnacht* – the night of the broken glass – the Nazis' orgy of murder and wanton destruction. Later we were to learn that 91 Jews had been slain in the night, and thousands more savagely beaten. More than 30,000 were arrested on trumped up charges and sent to the camps at Dachau, Sachsenhausen and Buchenwald.

Mutti's initial reluctance to heed the milkman's warning was typical of the way so many people felt: everyone could see what was going on under the Nazis, but no one wanted to believe it. Many of them were highly intelligent people – bankers, big industrialists, scholars – yet they refused to accept the evidence that was everywhere around them. Possibly they thought a lot about it, but they certainly did not act on it. Much later, safe in England, I discussed this many, many times with Papa. I would say: "Why – when you saw all these things that were going on – did you stay? Why did you not get out earlier?"

His answer was that life was comfortable, despite the harassment. He had a wonderful home, his business was flourishing, all his friends were in Berlin, and none of them believed it.

After the milkman had gone, Mutti and Papa got dressed and went downstairs to find out what had happened. They learned that the windows had been smashed in every synagogue in Germany. Anything that was known to be Jewish – shops, banks, cafes – was similarly vandalised and looted. Among the 7,000 businesses attacked was "Israel," one of the biggest warehouses in Berlin. But here the Nazis had blundered, for "Israel" was owned by British Jews. There was an immediate outcry by the Foreign Office in London, and Hitler, anxious to keep appeasement talks going with Prime Minister Neville Chamberlain, was forced to have every single shattered pane, every splintered door in the warehouse made good as new.

Kristallnacht was the final blow. After that, the people who did not believe it or could not believe it, or would not believe it, at last saw what was happening all around them. They began to plan their escape.

And yet I still cannot fathom why Papa waited so long. After all, he had already experienced the narrowest of escapes not long before *Kristallnacht*.

I remember it quite vividly. It was a Friday night in the early autumn of 1938 and the family was gathered, awaiting Papa's return from his business. We were already looking forward to our traditional *Shabbos* meal, followed by his stories.

But this night something went wrong. Papa did not come home.

Even as children we did not need to be told what had happened. He had been caught in a police dragnet. We all looked to Mutti, hoping for reassurance. I recall that she was if anything quieter than usual. She shooed us out of the room while she rang her friends to see if anyone knew what had happened to Papa. At length a sketchy story emerged. It was just as Mutti had feared. Shortly after he had closed his shop in the Potzdammer Platz and set off home, he had run into a police unit. He had been arrested and locked up in a holding centre. The next stop was Buchenwald or one of the camps which had begun to spring up around Berlin. There was no charge against Papa, save that he was a Jew.

We were a very muted family that night. We even wept quietly – all except Mutti. She sat in her armchair, deep in thought. We were anxious not to disturb her and so we tiptoed off to bed very troubled in our minds. No one had to spell out what would happen to Papa. In a day or so he would be sent to a "labour camp"; our only view of him would be through the razor wire. This is what had already happened to so many thousands of innocent Jews. And not one of them, not a single man, had ever been returned to his family.

We four children awoke to a grey and cheerless morning. But if we were downcast, Mutti was just the opposite. She was brisk and purposeful as she moved about the apartment and her eyes were bright with determination.

I think it was Siche who asked her: "What are you going to do, Mutti?"

And Mutti, donning her smartest coat and hat, said: "I am going to fetch your father. I'm not coming home without him."

It was an incredible statement yet she meant every word of it. The *Shabbos* was not over but off she went, a small yet determined figure. She insisted on going alone. We waited wracked by doubt. How could anyone as gentle, as tender as our Mutti even hope to make the Nazis free Papa? But we also knew how obstinate she could be. She would simply not be fobbed off or frightened by their uniforms and their power. We veered between impossible hope and darkest despair.

The waiting hours dragged by. It was dusk before we heard the key rattle in the front door. Instantly we all rushed into the hall and there was Mutti with a triumphant smile lighting her face. And there beside her was Papa. Our relief and happiness were indescribable. We had our Papa back. Suddenly the apartment was again full of whoops and laughter. We smothered them both in tearful hugs and kisses. Mutti had accomplished the impossible. She had brought our beloved Papa home.

It was only afterwards that we realised how utterly drained Mutti and Papa were. They were under no illusions about what would have happened to him had she not fought for his freedom.

Later Mutti would tell how she had armed herself with as much money as she could find before setting off to police headquarters and, bribing one official after another, she eventually bought Papa's way out. I don't think it was quite as simple as that. I firmly believe that Mutti's tenacity and her grit were the true currency that freed Papa.

All her life she remained quietly proud of what she had achieved, a feat which no-one else ever matched. On the occasion of her 80th birthday we held a big party for her and Mutti made a little speech in which she referred back to her role in the great escape. But her pride in her great achievement was nothing compared to our pride in her.

THE CODE OF THE FELDERS

Once a week, Papa held a card session in the *Herrenzimmer*. The game he and his companions played was Sixty-six, which has certain similarities to gin rummy. The purpose of the game is to make the cards in your hand add up to sixty-six. It was the only card game which that generation played. The other three players were usually Mr. Felder, a very wealthy businessman, Mr. Garten, a merchant, and Mr Reiss, a leading cigar wholesaler. Curiously Mr. Reiss never smoked cigars, but the blue smoke from his pipe drifted lazily over the table as they played.

The four friends played for money, but the stakes were very modest and if at the end of the evening, one man had won five reichsmarks, he had been remarkably lucky indeed. The true purpose of these sessions was not to play cards, but to talk about the state of affairs. It was no longer safe to talk openly in cafes or on the street, because one never knew who might be listening. Even the telephone could not be trusted because the Gestapo had begun to bug the lines of Jewish families. Letters were intercepted as a matter of course and a careless word, a slight indiscretion, was enough to warrant a midnight raid and immediate arrest. And so the only times friends could meet to say what they were truly thinking was on occasions like these card sessions.

The faces of Papa and his three friends were always lined with anxiety, and even when they played they did not relax.

As I said earlier, I loved to do my homework in the *Herrenzimmer*, and often I was in my usual place on the settee when Papa and his companions were playing. I kept very quiet and I suppose after a time they forgot I was there.

I can still remember the slap of the cards on Papa's desk and the jubilant cry as one or other player shouted: "Sixty-six!" followed by the rueful groans of the losers.

Between games, the four sat hunched over the desk, sipping lemon tea and nibbling cake and discussing the worsening situation. I never eavesdropped on what they were saying, but very often my mind wandered from my work and I overheard snatches of the players' conversation. One evening I chanced to hear Mr Felder talking about his plans for the future. It didn't mean anything to me, but my memory, which has always been a magpie at collecting useless scraps of information, filed it away. And that useless scrap was to prove wonderfully useful several years later.

The conversation that particular night concerned the plans each of the four players was making to protect his savings. Papa had already told us his was lodged with the Central Bank in Prague and apparently safely beyond the Nazis' grasp. For no one foresaw the invasion of Czechoslovakia. Papa had placed the money in a special coded account which had a password rather than a number, so that our young minds would remember it better. In our case the password was Feige-Perel-Sara-Gitel, the combination of Paula's and my Jewish names. For the first thing a good Jewish father did was to ensure that his daughters would be well provided with dowries.

Time after time Papa had made us recite the password. He wanted to be certain that if anything happened to him, we could claim our inheritance.

That night in the *Herrenzimmer*, Mr. Felder, the wealthiest of the four players, disclosed he had been thinking along similar lines. He had just returned from Switzerland which was the preferred repository by Jewish businessmen. Like Papa, he did not trust his sons to remember a numbered account, therefore he had placed his savings – a very large sum of money – in a coded account with the Bank Leu in Zurich. He had devised a password based on his sons' names. (Unfortunately it later transpired that he did not tell them the details of the account.)

I heard all this and promptly forgot it until one day in 1946. By this time we were living in London, as was Mr. Reiss's son, Simon. He was a close friend of both Mr. Felder's boys who were now American citizens and serving in the US army. They happened to be passing through London and they called in on Simon. Mr. Felder had not been able to escape Germany, and he, alas, was among those who perished in the camps.

His two sons candidly admitted they had lost everything in Germany. There was not a trace of their father's fortune. One of them said: "We know our father had a lot of money in Switzerland, but we have no idea of which bank, which name, which number." Simon Reiss had a brainwave. He suggested: "Let's ask Mr. Neuwirth whether he knows what happened to the money."

So the three of them – Mr. Felder's sons in their G.I. uniforms – came round to our house in Hampstead. Papa heard their story and shook his head sadly: "I know there is money in Switzerland because your father told me so. But I'm sorry, I have no idea where it might be."

At this point my magpie memory came to the rescue.

"I know," I said. Jaws dropped, eyes widened with surprise.

I said: "It's in the Bank Leu in Switzerland. And it's under a password based on your names."

The outcome of that was the boys went to Switzerland, told their story and, as a result, were rewarded with their rightful inheritance within a matter of weeks.

But tens of thousands of other Jews were denied theirs. It is only now, almost sixty years on, that the Swiss Government is setting out to repay the so-called Nazi Gold – the billions of reichsmarks lodged in its banks, the precious savings of people like Mr. Felder.

I often think back to those card sessions in the *Herrenzimmer* in the autumn of 1938. Papa's good friend Mr. Reiss, the cigar merchant, like Mr. Felder, died in a camp. Both men were German Jews and could not obtain passports to freedom. But Mr. Garten and his wife miraculously evaded the Nazis and fled across the border into Belgium. There they found refuge with a Gentile family who kept the couple hidden throughout the War. Earlier the Gartens had managed to send their sons and daughter, Jeffrey, Joe and Celia, to the relative safety of England.

Neither the boys nor Celia knew anything of the escape and they truly believed their parents had died like so many others. The Gartens' children were free and safe but there was no joy in their freedom. In truth, they were in deep mourning.

Jeffrey joined the British Army to fight against the people he believed had murdered his parents. Celia, although she was in her late teens, therefore several years older than me, became a very close friend. She was like one of our own family and lived with us in

Hampstead in the final years of the War. There was much laughter in that house, but Celia's laughter was often tempered by the tragic loss of her parents.

When the War ended, all over Europe there were hundreds of thousands of refugees all desperately trying to locate their families. It was a massive undertaking and the Magen David Adom – the Jewish Red Cross – and the International Red Cross played vital roles in knitting together unravelled families wherever they could. It was through these efforts that one day a letter addressed to Celia arrived at our house. It told her that the parents who had kissed her goodbye seven long years ago were alive and well.

The memory of that joyous moment lives with me still.

THE SNIPER IN
SHORT TROUSERS

In July, 1938, Siche had his thirteenth birthday. It was time for his Bar Mitzvah, and a great deal of fuss was made over him. I was always aware that ours was a large family, but I never realised quite how extensive it was until the Bar Mitzvah day. There were so many aunts, uncles, cousins and second cousins there to celebrate Siche's passage to manhood.

I remember the synagogue was packed as Siche, looking very dashing in his new sailor suit, stood up to read from the Torah. An unruly lock of brown hair flopped across his forehead. Otherwise he looked very grown up indeed and we were all hugely proud of him.

Mutti and Papa marked the occasion with lunch for all the guests and later an evening reception in our apartment. In earlier years a party like this would have been held in a hotel or function hall, but it was now no longer safe for Jews to congregate in any public place in Germany.

Naturally the guests all had presents for the Bar Mitzvah boy – clothes, toys, books, games – our apartment was an Aladdin's cave of treats for him.

But there were two undoubted star gifts in Siche's collection. The first was a bicycle, but no ordinary bicycle. This was a state-of-the-art machine, with a brightly-chromed frame, swept-back handlebars and a bell which he never tired of ringing.

Siche made it clear from the outset that this was *his* special bike. His and his alone. He issued dark threats about what he would do to us if we dared lay a finger on it. And just to make sure that the temptation was placed beyond our reach, he constructed an elaborate pulley of chains suspended from the ceiling of his bedroom. When the bicycle was not in use, he locked it in the chains and hoisted it several feet off the floor. Paula, Myer and I could frequently be found in Siche's bedroom, gazing with hungry eyes at this wonderful machine. Siche graciously allowed us to look at it.

The second prized present was equally his exclusive property. It was an air rifle with a beechwood stock and, in the centre of its barrel, a framed sight. It fired little steel balls, as bright as quicksilver. Siche was tall for his age, but even so, this gun seemed far too big for any child.

In the weeks after his Bar Mitzvah, Siche had a set programme when he returned from school. He would winch down his bike from the ceiling, collect his air rifle from whichever secret corner he had hidden it, and cycle down to the *Ufer*, the banks of the Spree.

This was a large open area, mainly given over to allotments, but there was also plenty of space for children to play. Here Siche would set up tin cans or draw cardboard targets and practise his sharpshooting skills. He rapidly became very good at it. Just how good, we would very soon find out.

Our bedrooms opened out onto a long terrace overlooking the street and we used the terrace as our very own playground. It was here we raced our scooters and chased each other. In the autumn of 1938 Siche could often be seen here, aiming his precious air rifle at imaginary targets.

This is how I found him one early afternoon, just after lunch. It was a warm day and he was wearing shorts and a light sweater. He was leaning on the balcony outside the room Paula and I shared, and aiming his gun in the general direction of the street, four storeys below. I can't say I was paying too much attention because I was involved in my own amusement.

But I do remember looking over the balcony and seeing far below two uniformed SS officers conducting an interrogation in the street. I was looking at them when suddenly, to my left, I heard the CRACK! of the air rifle and to my incredulous horror I saw one of the officers crumple in a heap on the pavement. Realisation dawned on me instantly.

Siche had just shot an SS man.

I turned to look at Siche and he was drained of all colour. We were both paralysed for a moment and then we dashed through the French windows into the apartment shrieking "Mutti!" at the tops of our voices.

Mutti emerged from the lounge to see what all the fuss was about. Myer and Paula, hearing our yells, came running. One look at our panic-stricken faces told them this was more than routine mischief.

"What is it?" she asked.

I was still so shocked I couldn't tell her. Siche, shivering with fright, blurted out: "I've shot an SS man."

"You did *what?*"

Siche swallowed hard and told her again.

Mutti put a hand to her brow. "Oh, my God, Siche. It's not true."

I nodded dumbly. It was true. She went to the window and looked out. The wounded man was lying on the pavement clutching his knee. His fellow SS officer was staring up at the apartments. He seemed to be looking straight at us.

It was all too horribly true. Our own little Bar Mitzvah boy had just shot one of Hitler's elite.

Mutti, as I've mentioned before, always somehow kept her head no matter how great the crisis. And this was her finest hour. In an instant she was brisk and businesslike.

"Quick, Siche. Run down the backstairs. Do not let anyone see you. Run directly to your Aunt Ella. Do not stop. Do not tell anyone else what you have done."

Siche, for the very first time in his life, was prepared to obey Mutti's every word.

She continued. "When you get to Aunt Ella's, you must stay there. Do not go out. Do not come home."

He was still clutching the mighty air rifle. Mutti took it from his grasp and propelled him to the back stairs. "Now go!" she ordered.

Siche leapt down those stairs like a mountain goat. He never looked back. Paula, Myer and I watched him go. Our eyes were wide with shock.

Mutti ran upstairs with the offending air rifle and buried it under the soiled laundry in the wash room. In a moment she was back. She said to us: "Remember, you know nothing."

She sat down in the kitchen, her face devoid of any anxiety, her dark eyes unclouded of worry. We tried to copy her poise.

Together we waited for the knock on the door.

❖ ❖ ❖

We did not have long to wait, perhaps no more than ten minutes, but those were the longest minutes I've ever lived through. We all felt the same.

Every now and then one of us would run to the dining room window – we dared not show ourselves on the balcony – and call back a report to the others.

"The ambulance has arrived."

"There are two police cars."

"They're putting him on a stretcher."

"The street is full of police."

"The SS man looks badly wounded."

"They're looking up here."

In between these bulletins we thought about what would happen to us, and, more particularly, to Siche. What would the SS do to a Jewish boy who shot one of their officers? These men were Heinrich Himmler's pride and joy, Hitler's most fanatical disciples. The punishment was too dreadful to contemplate.

"They're running into the block."

We heard their angry voices in the stairwell and the sound of their fists hammering on the doors of our neighbours. The din grew closer and closer. And then they were pounding on our door.

Mutti smoothed the folds of her dress and sat primly waiting while Bianca went to answer their summons. We heard the barked command from the hall: "Fetch your mistress, immediately." Bianca reappeared in the dining room. There was no need for her to say anything. Mutti arose without haste and went out to face the SS. We children sat in the dining room and stared open-mouthed at each other. My throat was so dry, it was painful to swallow.

Down the hallway we heard the sound of Mutti's even voice.

"Yes? Can I help you?"

But politeness was no defence against a squad of SS men, hellbent on revenge. They stormed into the apartment. We looked up apprehensively to see the doorway to the dining room full of black uniforms.

What the officers saw was three unnaturally quiet Jewish children, staring back at them with big round eyes and pale, frightened faces. Someone more intelligent than they might have guessed that our expressions were an open admission of guilt. Fortunately the SS assumed our fear was merely the standard reaction to their menace. None of us looked like a sniper.

They lost interest in us and began turning the apartment upside down. Mutti followed them from room to room, asking in aggrieved tones: "What are you looking for? What has happened?"

The senior officer told her: "One of my men has been shot by someone in these apartments. Do you have a gun?"

"A gun?" Mutti smiled disbelievingly. "Of course I don't have a gun."

The officer looked at her. Mutti, with her fashionable clothes and soft voice hardly fitted his image of an urban guerrilla. She looked precisely what she was: a respectable middle-class mother with three scared children trailing behind her.

The SS consulted their lists. They knew exactly who lived in which apartment. Where was her husband? Where was Siche?

Mutti answered without hesitation. Papa was at his office, Siche at a friend's house doing his school work. There was not the faintest tremor in her voice to suggest she was covering up.

Yet all the time she must have been absolutely terrified that one of the SS men might venture upstairs to the laundry room and find the gun.

The squad moved out, leaving her with a final warning: if she knew anything about the shooting, it was her duty as a responsible citizen to inform them. If she failed to do so...

We heard their boots echo down the stairs. We risked a glimpse over the balcony. On the street a handful of SS men were quizzing passers-by. The police cars and the trucks began to move out. Soon even the SS were gone.

In the lounge we at last expelled a sigh of relief, a sigh you could have heard in the Tiergarten.

Siche meanwhile had done precisely as he had been instructed. He was now safely under wraps in Aunt Ella's house in the Flensburger Strasse where she had a fruit and greengrocery store.

My aunt had nine children of her own, but the three eldest boys had earlier that year gone to Russia, deeming it safer there than in Berlin. This fact gave Siche an immediate cover story: if the SS came calling, Aunt Ella could pretend that Siche was one of her own sons.

He told her precisely what he had done and she effectively placed him under house arrest, for she recognised that Siche must to all intents and purposes vanish.

This enforced curfew must have grated sorely on the young marksman. Though I imagine that what grieved him most was he could no longer shoot his beloved air rifle or go riding on his jealously-guarded bicycle.

Back at No. 21 Agricola Strasse, we were experiencing some drastic changes too. Papa came home from a busy day at the office to find his world falling to pieces. Mutti, tearful and wringing her hands, sobbed out the terrible story of Siche's misdeeds. In the circumstances, any father could be forgiven for ranting and raving about his son's moment of sheer lunacy. But Papa knew that this was no time for recriminations. The first priority was to protect Siche.

He and Mutti closeted themselves in the lounge and debated what to do. They were in there for a couple of hours and when they emerged, I had never seen Papa look so grave. Mutti, seeing our anxious faces, said: "Don't worry. Everything will be all right."

I don't think we were entirely convinced.

Papa retired to the *Herrenzimmer* and placed a long distance phone call to his nephew, Rafuel Margolis, in England. He had an urgent favour to seek. Papa asked him if he could enrol Siche immediately in the Talmudical College in Gateshead. Rafuel did not need to ask why this sudden request. All he knew was that Siche must get to England as soon as possible. Rafuel replaced the phone and began making arrangements.

Gradually our parents' plan became clear. From that night on we ceased to have a big brother. We were warned not to talk about Siche's exploit, not even to our closest chums, for one stray remark could jeopardize his very life.

I'm not sure what happened to the gun but I imagine that sometime that night, when we children were asleep, Papa went to the laundry room and retrieved it. Then under cover of darkness, he spirited it out of the apartment and dumped it. He never told us where it went, but I have a sneaking suspicion it might still be lying in the mud at the bottom of the Spree.

Siche, as I say, had effectively ceased to exist. Our apartment block was under constant surveillance, so neither Mutti nor Papa dared visit him in case they were followed. Their only contact with their wayward son was through messages whispered in the ears of

trusted friends and duly relayed to Siche in his bolthole on the
Flensburger Strasse.

Our whole future was now clouded with doubt. There was only
one absolute certainty: the SS would not give up their hunt for the
sniper. And so it proved.

First thing next morning another cluster of black uniforms
mustered on the pavement where the officer had been shot. They
were joined by police and by men with strange equipment. They
drew a chalk mark on the spot where the SS man had fallen. His
uninjured partner was there to make sure they got it right. He kept
gesticulating at our apartment block. Clearly he was absolutely
convinced that the shot had been fired from there. Every so often he
scanned the balconies through binoculars. Somehow the binoculars
always seemed to come to rest on our terrace.

The other officers went about their work painstakingly. They
made calculations, drew possible trajectories, estimated the range.
They went away, only to return the next day, and the next.

And then one morning I looked over the balcony and I saw they
had reached a conclusion. They were all staring at the block, and
every single eye was focussed on our apartment.

Soon Mutti found herself summoned to the door again. This
time the SS were insistent. "We *know* the shot came from here."

Mutti stood her ground. Politely and patiently she insisted:
"There must be some mistake. We do not have a gun."

They searched every corner, including the laundry room, but
they found nothing – the little silver bullets had also vanished – nor
could they shake Mutti's calm demeanour. I had never thought my
mother possessed any acting skills, but her performance that
morning deserved an Oscar. Mutti knew her son's life depended on
her, and she played her role to perfection. If for one moment she had

broken down under that relentless interrogation and confessed that Siche was guilty of a foolish prank, that would have been sufficient for the SS to hunt him down and shoot him.

The inquisitors went away, but they had not given up.

We children were unaware of it, but Papa's plan to send Siche to safety was already well advanced. A letter arrived from England offering Siche a place at the Talmudical College. That was essential for him to gain entry into Britain. And one other vital piece of documentation was already in place. A few years earlier, Papa, with commendable foresight, had taken out individual passports for all of us. Even little Myer had his own passport. These papers gave our nationality as Czech, and as such we were less likely to be prevented from leaving the country.

The next problem was rather more complex. Neither Mutti nor Papa wanted to send their 13-year-old son alone on a long journey to a foreign country. This is where a remarkable organisation came to our aid. Jewish groups in Britain had long been petitioning the Home Office to grant a mass visa to groups of children from central Europe. Eventually, in the late autumn of 1938, Britain gave the go ahead for the young immigrants, but with the proviso that a £50 bond was posted for each child. If one remembers that a house then cost around £400, it can be seen that £50 represented several thousand in today's money. But the bonds were forthcoming and within days, the first *Kindertransport* was on its way, carrying 600 children from Vienna to new homes in England.

The *Kindertransport* refugees were drawn from those who were most at risk, the young German and Austrian Jews. Austria earlier

Our last winter on the slopes of the Ice Cream Mountain – Mutti and Papa, with me on the left, and Paula and Myer.

that year had been annexed by the Nazis and its Jewish people were subject to the same draconian laws as those in Germany. Therefore children from these two communities took priority on the *Kindertransport*.

But the Refugee Children's Movement was only too happy to look after a Czech Jew on his way west. There was one simple condition, which Papa and Mutti were delighted to meet: Once in England, Siche must hand over his precious Czech passport to the Movement. It could then be smuggled back to Berlin and used to let a German boy escape. Papa also gave the Movement money so that others could be helped to freedom.

The first *Kindertransport* left Berlin on December 12, 1938. Siche was not actually part of it because that would have meant taking away some other child's place. But he was on the same train and the Refugee Children's Movement carers promised to look after him on the long journey to England. Aunt Ella took Siche to the station for a tearful farewell. Papa and Mutti went too, but they had to keep their emotions in check for the Nazis were still hunting the phantom sniper of the Agricola Strasse. If the SS had seen my parents tearfully bundle their son out of the country, they would know they had their suspect.

We children were not allowed to come and say goodbye to our big brother for we would have been sure to give the game away. All we could do was to send our love for Papa and Mutti to whisper to him. They were forced to pretend they were Siche's uncle and aunt. It was a strained goodbye which must have cost my parents dear. They held back the tears as the great locomotive pulled out of the station, taking away their first-born child.

MAZEL

On the day I was born there was another happy event in Papa's life. One of his debtors paid up. A rare event indeed.

The year, it must be remembered, was 1929 and Germany was still in the throes of hyper-inflation, when a single loaf of bread could cost as much as a man earned in a month.

At that time the most common currency in any business transaction was a *Wechsel*, in effect a bill of exchange. The *Wechsel* was signed and agreed in all good faith. But the economy was in such turmoil that debtors found themselves simply unable to pay. In his office Papa had a drawer full of *Wechsel* notes which were literally not worth the paper they had been written on.

And then quite out of the blue, Papa found himself with a new daughter – and a paying customer. There was only one word for it: *Mazel*.

Mazel means many things. It can be fortune, or serendipity, or simply being in the right place at the right time. I suppose the easiest definition is luck.

Papa took one look at his redeemed *Wechsel* and pronounced that it was a lucky omen for his infant daughter, that she would have a lucky star over her. Papa was an astute businessman with his feet very much on the ground, but he always firmly believed that *Mazel* had played a mysterious part in his success.

He told Mutti: "Now Susi has inherited my *Mazel*."

As I grew up, he told me the same story many times over. Looking back over my life, I think how right he was. I do not talk about the future, for that is surely tempting fate. I am thinking only of the past.

And in 1938 it seemed as though my *Mazel* was working overtime.

Now that Siche was gone there was an unfillable gap in the family. We sorely missed everything about him, even his boisterous mischief-making. And even as children we knew he would never come back to our home in Berlin. His beloved bicycle dangled in its chains in his empty bedroom.

What we didn't know was that Siche's exploits with the air rifle had also hastened *our* departure. As 1938 closed and the terrible year of 1939 dawned, Papa was finally coming to accept that we all must flee. Siche's letters from England told us that he was happy and, perhaps even more importantly, that he was safe. Papa looked again at the life we were forced to live under the Nazis – the routine harassment, the round-ups, the ostracism (Jewish children were now banned from playing in public parks) – and he began plotting a way out for his children. He decided that Paula and I must be next to go. In the distant unimaginable town of Gateshead, Siche was detailed to find new homes for his sisters. It was a very responsible task to place upon the shoulders of a wayward 13-year-old boy. But the very first thing the Nazis took from Jewish children was their childhood. Siche, to his eternal credit, responded magnificently.

The preparations in Berlin were intense and thorough. On the 23rd of December I turned nine. I felt very grown up. There was a party of course, and lots of friends, but it was different without Siche. I cannot remember what presents I was given but soon afterwards both Paula and I found ourselves the proud possessors of new navy double-breasted coats, made from the finest cloth Papa could find. These wonderfully warm coats came equipped with huge turn-ups on the hems and cuffs. The shoulders and waist could be similarly let out to fit a rapidly growing girl. But the cut was so generous I felt I could have doubled my height and my girth overnight and there would still be plenty of room.

We were presented with new boots, gloves, scarves and knitted woollen hats in navy and white. We tried on our ensembles before the bedroom mirror and were mightily pleased with ourselves. Looking back at us were two assured and sophisticated young ladies of the world.

We had smart black suitcases for our books and clothes. And we had matching handbags. This was the accessory which gave me the greatest delight. It was fashioned from leather so supple, so fine, that one had only to touch it to feel the sheer quality.

The lining was of watered silk. The stitching was meticulous. One would never guess that under the fine stitching lay a secret compartment containing ten pounds in English money. It sounds very little now but it added up to a great deal then.

Papa had also contacted the Refugee Children's Movement again and set in motion the same travel arrangements that he had made for Siche. Again it was agreed that we would be looked after by the *Kindertransport* volunteers, but we would not be part of the mass visa. And Papa repeatedly stressed to us that we must give the RCM our Czech passports as soon as we had reached England. His face solemn, he counselled Paula and me: "Remember, your passports mean two other little girls will also escape."

This was a time I suppose I should remember with perfect clarity. Poor Mutti must have been devastated. She had already said goodbye to her elder son. Soon she was to see her daughters leave. She, Papa and little Myer were to stay behind in the nightmare that had become Berlin. At least for the time being. Her own mother and father were patiently awaiting their British entry papers, without knowing if they would ever arrive.

Mutti's family was exceptionally close. Never a week passed without her calling in on Oma and Opa, and our aunts and uncles were forever visiting us, or vice versa. Now Mutti was facing the heartrending break up of her family. God alone knows how she found the strength to cope in that dark winter.

As I say, I should remember all this. To my shame, what I remember most clearly is the sense that Paula and I were about to embark on a truly wonderful adventure. We counted off the days to our departure. It mattered not to us that we were going to a new life in a town which was barely a dot on the map. Gateshead. We giggled as we practised saying it: "Gateshead." It sounded romantic to our childish ears.

The days sped by in a flurry of preparation. There were so many friends to bid farewell. We cried often, yet always at the back of our minds was the magical thought that we would soon be off to a distant shore where all sorts of marvellous experiences lay in store for us.

And so bright and early on the morning of the 18th of January, 1939, we woke and dressed. Our cases were already prepared the night before, but that didn't stop Bianca rushing into our room every few moments just to make sure we had everything we needed. In between these little panics, she would dash to the kitchen and prepare sandwiches for us to eat on the train.

Papa had a long list of details. Mutti brushed my hair and talked softly to me about the journey ahead. "Now, don't worry. You will be safe."

Paula asked: "Tonight we will be in Holland?"

Mutti smiled gently: "Tonight you will be boarding a ship for England."

A ship! Paula and I looked at each other, barely able to hold back our excitement. We had never been on anything bigger than a rowing boat. The prospect was just too mouth-watering.

I suppose in our girlish exuberance we were unaware of the silence we would leave behind. It is only when one becomes a mother that one realises.

Myer was devastated that he could not come to the station to wave us farewell. "Please, *please*," he begged tearfully. Papa was gentle but firm. "I'm sorry Myer, but there will be too many people there."

Our little brother sulked. We tried to make Papa relent. But he was quite adamant. "Myer stays with Bianca," he said.

What none of us knew was that Papa was simply protecting Myer from the awful scene which he knew lay in store at the station. Looking back, I am so glad that Papa refused to let him see us off on the train.

As we said our goodbye to the apartment, Bianca squeezed us to her bosom and made us promise her we would look after each other. Those were the last words Bianca ever said to us.

We set off for the station, Paula and I so proud of ourselves in our new coats with the handbags swinging at our shoulders. If anything, our parents encouraged our high spirits. Certainly, they never showed for one moment the loss they were feeling.

It was only when we joined the throng in the Berlin *Hauptbahnhof* that we glimpsed the terrible price parents were forced to pay.

I will try to be as dispassionate as I can. The train detailed for the *Kindertransport* was on a platform off to one side, as if it were isolated. Its very presence signified freedom for the children, anguish for their parents. But to reach the promised sanctuary of the platform, one had to brave the cordon of SS, police and bureaucrats. They examined every scrap of paper. They searched every bag. They scrutinized the faces of every parent. And every child.

All this we could have dealt with, but what made the ordeal so appalling was the heartrending grief, as mothers, fathers, children all wept together at their parting. The children knew only that they were leaving their parents. The parents knew they would never, *never* see their children again. This was not a farewell. This was a last goodbye.

The great vaulted ceiling of the *Hauptbahnhof* reverberated and magnified that awful moment. There were perhaps 200 children destined for the train. Some of them only three, four, five years old. Great big men in SS black came and stared into little tear-stained faces. The men had guns, they had menace, they had absolute power over life and death. Paula and I fell silent as we edged closer and closer to the cordon. Beside us, Mutti and Papa repeated over and over again: "Don't worry. They are only checking the documents."

Ah, but they were doing more than that. They were looking for any minor discrepancy which would give them an excuse to refuse a passport to freedom for any one of us.

Occasionally they found such a trivial error. Perhaps a child whose birthplace had been misspelt, or whose name did not quite match his papers. When they detected one, this hapless, bewildered child would turn to his parents who would spill out their grief even louder than before. And that in turn made the child yet more distraught. He could not understand why his parents were so anxious to send him away. They, poor people, knew his return meant that he too would perish.

Yet while all this was going on, the great station was still functioning as if this were just another normal day. On the other side of the cordon busy Berliners came and went. They must have been aware of the awful tableau taking place beside them. Perhaps they simply turned their heads away. I would like to think they averted their eyes in shame.

Every child, regardless of how humble his or her background, was dressed in the smartest clothes. Each had a shiny new suitcase to hold a few precious belongings. Many parents had begged and borrowed to pay for these new outfits. They knew they were sending their child to another life in another land, and they went hungry themselves to make certain their child was immaculately turned out.

By now Mutti and Papa, Paula and I were all crying. I sobbed into Papa's coat as he held me close and whispered: "Be brave, Susi. We will join you soon in England."

Papa had never lied to us. When he said we would all be together again, I knew it was true.

Then we were at the cordon. Papa handed over our documents. A guard took my grey Czech passport and studied the details. He made a curt gesture towards an official who was standing by with a big sheaf of cardboard rectangles. The official copied my name onto one of the cards. He wrote: "Susi Neuwirth, born Berlin, December 23, 1929. Age 9." Then he hung the card on a piece of string around my neck. Paula's passport also survived the scrutiny, and she too was supplied with a label.

We huddled together in fear – so many little bundles with a tag round each neck, like so many items of freight. I looked around at the other children. "Schlomo Hahn, born Munich, October 14, 1933. Age 5," "Annette Schonfield, born Cologne, August 1935. Age 3." These were little childish faces which in a more civilised land would be clear-eyed and smiling. Now they were pinched and frightened. Some were desperately clinging to a well-worn toy or a favourite doll. Every child had a handkerchief and every handkerchief was drenched with tears. And these children were the fortunate ones.

Our new suitcases were searched, then taken from us and stored in the luggage wagon. We were really going. Through our tears Paula and I smiled wanly at each other and held hands. The SS began to harry us along the platform. I turned once and waved a last frantic farewell to Mutti and Papa, for they were not allowed on to the platform. They soon vanished behind a black wall of uniforms. As we began to board the train, the wails of the bereaved parents rose to a crescendo. It was so loud, so prolonged, that it drowned even the noise of the locomotive as it built up steam.

It was a corridor train and, with Paula leading the way, we found a compartment. Ahead of us lay a journey of close on 300 miles before we crossed the Dutch border, but until then we were helpless refugees in a hostile country. The Nazis never let us forget it. As the train rolled west through the snowy fields and forests of Havelland, the cries of our fellow travellers continued unabated.

Every now and then the door to our compartment slid open and a guard would demand to search our handbags. They found Bianca's sandwiches, the toys, the addresses of friends we had promised to write to. But they never found the English money stitched into the silken lining.

But there were welcome visitors too, the volunteer workers from the Refugee Children's Movement. Throughout that nightmare journey they flitted from compartment to compartment, drying someone's eyes here, lulling a child to sleep there. They too were constantly harassed and chivvied by the SS, but the women from the RCM continued to go about their work with unflagging love and tenderness.

They were all too aware that before very long almost every child on that train of tears would be an orphan.

Indeed, of all the young passengers, Paula and I were the only children who ever saw their parents again.

EXODUS

The wearisome day drew on and as night spilled across the frost-bitten landscape, it gradually dawned on Paula and me that we were not the sophisticated young ladies of the world we had so admired in our bedroom mirror. We were just two lonely children, a long way from home. In my head, I recited over and over again to the rhythm of the clacking wheels, my only words of English.

"My name is Susi. I am nine. I am from Berlin."

There was no comfort in the words. Every mile brought us closer to freedom and to a promised new life in England. This is what had filled our dreams and our every waking minute for weeks. Only this very morning we had set off for the station bubbling with excitement.

Yet what a sorry picture we painted now. I cannot remember which of us started crying first, but soon we were both sobbing grievously. I looked across at Paula and she seemed to have shrunk inside her stylish new coat. All I could see of her was a little round pale face with bitter tears coursing down her cheeks and onto her collar. I must have looked equally wretched.

For each passing mile was not bringing us closer to a dream: it was taking us away from the love and happiness that had surrounded us every second of our lives.

Paula said between her sobs: "We will never see our beautiful home again."

The realisation prompted a new wave of weeping.

We hugged each other for comfort. I said: "And we'll never go to the fleapit again."

Another tide of tears.

But neither of us dared confess the true dread in our treacherous hearts, that we might never again see our beloved Mutti and Papa and Myer. And so we cried about other things. Our lost friends, our room, our toys. At that very moment what we wanted most of all was to be snug in our beds, with Mutti and Papa kissing us goodnight. We wanted the simple love and security which we had always taken so much for granted.

But the great train hurtled on into the darkness and the unknown. So many happy scenes flooded my mind. Only last week we had said goodbye to Oma and Opa in their apartment on the Blumen Strasse. As a special treat Oma had baked for us *kichalech*, sweet biscuits filled with nuts, for she knew how we loved them.

Now clinging to each other in that rattling carriage Paula and I wept that we might never taste her *kichalech* again. What we were really saying was we might never again see our dear Oma and Opa.

There were so many such memories. One after another I bade them farewell. It was as if this monstrous train were stripping away our past, that we were all alone in the world, without family, without friends, without a future. And we cried.

Then suddenly the clacking iron wheels changed their rhythm. We were slowing down. The engine shuddered and came to a standstill. Through our tears we gazed out into the night. We had reached Aachen, the last stop before the border.

Over to the west we could see the lights of Holland. In the sharp winter air they glittered bright and pure like stars. We stared raptly at them and for a moment we forgot our desolation. Our dreamed-of freedom was only a moment away.

But we were still in the nightmare of Germany. Here a sullen yellow light bathed the border station. There were shadows on the platform. We cleared the condensation from the window so that we might see better. But when we saw what awaited us on the platform, we shrank back on the hard wooden seats. For even here, on the very edge of deliverance, there was a dark cluster of SS men.

The carriage doors were flung back and we heard the familiar sound of jackboots. Paula and I sat with our hands clenched so tightly together our knuckles were drained of blood. Further down the carriage we could make out the protesting voices of the RCM volunteers as they sought to protect their young charges from this final degradation.

I think Paula and I were aware even then that we just *had* to get across the frontier, we had to see the stars of that little town in Holland and the brighter world beyond. We were dry-eyed now. All our wailing and childish yearning was banished as in this one moment of utter dread we feared the Nazis might take away our dreams of freedom.

The same thought was in the minds of all the older children. As soon as the compartment doors smacked open to admit the SS, they choked back their tears. Obediently they handed over their papers for that last crucial inspection.

It didn't matter that these same papers had been pored over and pronounced valid by the SS in Berlin, nor that they had been painstakingly examined by officers on the train. All that mattered to us now was convincing these border guards that we had a right to leave Germany.

They took the Czech passports from Paula and me. Under law, the Germans had no right to detain Czech nationals, but the SS obeyed only their own law.

"Your bags," one officer demanded. There was no smile, no sympathy. His voice was sharp. This strange man hated us and I could not begin to understand why, but I expected nothing less. Another SS man flung all the suitcases off the luggage racks and rifled through our books and clothes.

We handed over the black handbags. Papa had supervised what we carried in them. There were no coins, for he didn't want as much as a pfennig to be stolen by the SS. For the same reason we did not have any jewellery, any item of value.

The sandwiches which Bianca had so lovingly prepared for us had long since been eaten. Now my bag contained little more than a hairbrush, a comb, a handkerchief and a handful of sweets. That and the crisp new English £10 note.

The officer upended the bag on the seat opposite and rooted through my few belongings. He turned his attention to the bag itself. My heart almost failed me. What if he found the money? It was all I had in the world. But once again the secret note went undetected. We were even made to turn out the contents of our voluminous pockets. There was nothing worth looting there either.

They gave us back our passports and turning away in disgust, the officers moved onto the neighbouring compartment and the prospect of better pickings. They left us to repack our belongings.

Paula and I looked at each other with suppressed excitement. We had cleared the final hurdle.

But even before we could savour the moment, something happened which plunged everyone's spirits back into the abyss. From further down the train we heard the clamour of voices. The SS had found some pretext to deny freedom to one of our fellow travellers. The journey ended here for this unfortunate child. The women of the RCM beseeched, cajoled, argued with the Nazis. But their entreaties counted for nothing.

Presently a little boy, sobbing piteously and with his cardboard placard still hanging from his neck, was escorted off the train between two huge SS men. One officer held his shoulder in a rough grasp, for the boy seemed incapable of walking. The women tried to follow him onto the platform but an armed guard blocked their way. Through the open window the women continued to plead for his return. But the child and his escort vanished into the dark shadows of the station.

A few moments later there was another commotion and a second child was bundled off the train. The women were crying now. These children had travelled so far and already suffered so much. For them to be taken away when liberty was literally in sight was a cruelty beyond belief.

Tonight in Berlin the parents of those children would be giving thanks that their son or daughter was safely out of the Nazis clutches. Tomorrow their children would be returned to them and the parents' cherished beacon of hope would be extinguished forever.

I later learned that every *Kindertransport* was subject to the same final gratuitous act of sadism by the SS. Two or three children were plucked from each group of young refugees and sent back to despair. There was never justification for the refusal. It simply gave the Nazis pleasure.

The guards finally completed their inspection and began to withdraw. Paula and I dared not look out of the window in case we drew their attention. We sat with our heads down, willing the train to move. Out on the platform we could hear boots crunching away from us through the snow. Then it went quiet. It seemed as if every single passenger was holding his breath.

There was maybe a moment of stark silence before the train's whistle rent the frozen air. The engine gave a deep sigh and slowly, ever so slowly, the platform began to slip away into the night. We were moving again.

We rolled across the border into Holland, uncertain at first whether to laugh or cry. Then realisation swept over us. We were out of Germany! We were safe! We could look from the windows. We could chatter. We could laugh. We could whoop with joy. We did all of those.

The flat plains of the border lands inched past and suddenly we were in Holland. In place of the dreaded swastika, Dutch flags were draped from the station and on the platform a reception committee awaited. There was a large group of women, their faces wreathed in smiles. There was also a substantial presence of men in uniforms, some with rifles at their shoulders.

But here was the most amazing thing.

These officers were smiling at us.

Paula and I were silent. In Berlin, any man in a uniform was our sworn enemy. We were used to taunts and insults and threats. That was the only way of life we knew. We were not used to smiles. We began to cry.

When eventually the *Kindertransport* children were shepherded off the train and onto Dutch soil, every one of us was completely drained. In the course of a single day we had experienced an astonishing roller coaster of emotions, from joy to despair, from excitement to loneliness, from an utter sense of fear to the sudden shock of freedom.

The very young children had to be carried off because they were fast asleep. They awoke to find themselves safe in the arms of cheery Dutch Jewish women. I don't have the words to express my eternal gratitude for these women and what they did for us. They held us to them while we spilled out our tears and fears. They crooned songs to the little ones. Most of all, they let us know we were no longer alone.

And when our tears were dried, they asked us if we were hungry. Hungry? I have never had such a hunger. The women had prepared a large warm hall for our arrival. In one corner vast pots of stew simmered. The tables were neatly laid out with bowls and spoons and bread. A large jolly woman ladled a helping of stew into my dish. The smell was mouthwatering. At the risk of being disloyal to Bianca's celebrated *tcholent*, this was a meal to remember.

Afterwards they brushed our hair and smartened us up for the next leg of the journey. Paula and I were not quite the sophisticated young ladies again, but we were no longer waifs. And so, after a last warm hug from the Dutch women, we boarded the train.

The German crew had been replaced and in their stead were the blue uniformed Dutch staff. They treated us as VIPs. We did not understand their language but their smiles let us know that the nightmare was finally over.

Paula and I were lulled to sleep by the rhythm of the train as it chugged its way through empty farmlands and sleeping villages.

The next thing I remember was being gently wakened by an RCM volunteer. The train had stopped. We were at the Hook of Holland. "Come on, Susi," she said. "It's time to get on the boat."

The boat. How excited we had been this morning at the thought of sailing across the North Sea in a boat. But that was a long time ago. If the woman had told me we were about to embark on a rocket to the moon, I couldn't have cared less. All I wanted to do was sleep.

It must have been a strange scene: 200 wearied children tottering or being carried up the steep gangway of the *De Praag* in the middle of the winter night. I don't remember it. All I can recall is placing my precious handbag under the pillow in my bunk, clambering between the crisp sheets, closing my eyes and giving myself up to sleep. Freedom could wait.

COLD COMFORT

The first sight of the promised land was less than promising. England was hidden behind a blanket of freezing fog. We stood by the bow peering out into the murk, our coat collars turned up against our ears. But even our wonderful coats were insufficient protection against the cold. The tips of Paula's ears and her nose were a raw red.

The ship edged almost imperceptibly through the sluggish grey waves. We knew we were near the harbour entrance because all around us we could hear the foghorns of other ships. Occasionally the dim grey outline of another vessel, as insubstantial as a ghost ship, would materialise briefly out of the peasouper before vanishing like a wraith.

A sailor in his dark blue uniform joined us in our vigil. "Harwich," he cheerfully announced, pointing at the wall of dirty yellow fog. He must have had X-ray vision, for we still couldn't see anything.

Even when the *De Praag* bumped softly against the quayside there was very little to see apart from the spectral arms of cranes looming out of the morning mist.

The RCM volunteers marshalled all the children and led us down the gangway. It was fearfully steep and I marvelled that we had been able to climb up it the night before.

We clattered ashore and into a cavernous grey building. The mood was strangely subdued for every child was locked in his or her own thoughts. We were going to new homes, with new parents, and the uncertainty of it all weighed heavily on us. But at least the customs officers and immigration people seemed good natured. I practised again my few words of introduction.

"My name is Susi. I am nine. I am from Berlin."

They were not needed, for my name, my age and the city were all there on the cardboard label around my neck.

Once we were through immigration, Paula and I handed our Czech passports to the RCM. It is one of life's little regrets that we never found out how they were later used, for we would dearly have loved to meet the other little girls smuggled out of Germany with our names around their necks and our passports in their bags.

After an interminable wait we boarded the train for London. London! The prospect brought cheer to our dampened spirits and we brightened up. But the overall atmosphere remained strangely solemn and we were on our best behaviour through the journey south. We gazed out of the windows to see what this new land looked like, but the fog blotted out everything, save the occasional bedraggled station and leafless tree.

The train pulled into Liverpool Street and a curiously restrained crocodile of children filed off, clutching smart new suitcases. We had been travelling non-stop for 24 hours. Here another reception committee awaited. Although I did not know it then, among the welcoming faces was that of Elaine Blond, the dynamo behind the Refugee Children's Movement. Her tenacity, compassion and diplomacy were to play a vital role in rescuing almost 10,000 children such as us from Hitler's clutches. In later years she was to become a special friend, whose generosity and kindness enriched everyone she touched.

Liverpool Street was the mustering point for all the new arrivals. It was also the point of dispersal. Among the waiting crowd were many couples who had volunteered to foster a child. They strained forward for the first glimpse of their new son or daughter. The children stared back a trifle warily. Only yesterday at this same time they had kissed *auf Wiedersehen* to their parents in Berlin. The younger children had absolutely no idea what lay in store for them: they believed they were simply having a holiday, for their parents could not bring themselves to tell them there would be no return.

We stood very quietly while one by one the names of the refugees were called out. This was the signal for their sponsors, the foster parents, to come forward and claim the child.

In an ideal world, all of the *Kindertransport* passengers would have gone to warm and loving homes. But life is rarely ideal, and the crowded platform at Liverpool Street yielded more than its fair share of unhappy endings. Some prospective foster parents had taken one quick glance at their intended charge and then simply melted away. Perhaps they thought the child was too plain or too delicate. Whatever the tawdry reason, these heartless people walked off, leaving a bewildered lonely child to cope with yet another blow: rejection. And there were some who merely wanted an unpaid skivvy, so if their nominated child appeared too frail, he or she was abandoned.

Several times a name was called out, only to be followed by a cruel silence. A little group of forlorn children gathered on the platform under the wing of an RCM volunteer.

But for others, there was a happy outcome. They were greeted by smiling couples who pressed toys and sweets into their hands. We watched the children's faces brighten as they went off with their new Muttis and Papas.

Our foster parents were still in Gateshead but at the station to meet us was Felix Sturm, a great friend of Siche's. They were the same age. Felix had got out of Berlin a few months earlier and Papa had arranged for him to be at Liverpool Street just so that there would be at least one familiar face to greet us. Felix had not come empty-handed. He presented us each with a huge bag of sweets and soon we were gossiping away about friends we had left behind. Felix was bright and breezy and his conversation did much to lift our spirits. I imagine the bag of sweets also helped.

It had been agreed that we would not go to Gateshead immediately because we needed to rest. There were dozens of children who had either not found sponsors or had another journey to make before reaching their destination, and we went with them to Bloomsbury House in central London.

This was the headquarters of the Jewish Refugee Association and it was used as a processing centre for all newcomers, adults and children. Our details were dutifully logged and that night we were transferred to the Jewish Temporary Shelter in London's East End. We were too young to appreciate it, but this was a rather historic building. It was founded at the turn of the century by Spanish and Portuguese Jews from the great banking families and it became the gateway to Britain for so many of our people from all over Europe.

The Shelter was right next door to the public baths and after a quick meal, we all trooped off for a very welcome and much needed bath.

Afterwards we got better acquainted with some of our fellow travellers. I made friends with Erika, a girl my own age, and, as was the custom of the day, we exchanged photographs. Erika tucked my snapshot away and said. "We must keep in touch." I think even then I knew there was very, very little likelihood of that. We were caught up in chaos and had absolutely no idea what the future held. But I took a photo from Erika and agreed, yes, we must write to each other.

This was the last photograph of me taken in Berlin. On my first night in England, I exchanged snapshots with another little girl who had travelled on the same Kindertransport. Fifty years later it resurfaced in the most astonishing circumstances.

Our evening meal yielded a few surprises. We were offered sliced white bread, which we had never seen before, and the tables were dotted with bowls of great fat Jaffa oranges. Another novel experience. We rather gorged ourselves on those.

That night however, as we lay chilled to the bone in the dormitory, we agreed there was one thing about England we didn't enjoy one little bit: it was absolutely *freezing*. We didn't get much sleep that first night because our shivering kept us awake.

We lay there between the chill sheets, our handbags under the pillows, and yearned for the warmth of our bedroom in the Agricola Strasse. How could anyone *live* in such a cold country?

What we didn't know at the time was that Britain was in the throes of one the most bitter winters since records began. What we also didn't know, fortunately, was that things were going to become a great deal colder.

"England is p-p-p-primitive," said Paula through chattering teeth.

"S-S-S-Stone Age," I agreed.

Perhaps this sounds as though we were being more than a little ungrateful to the country which had rescued us from the Nazis. But the truth is we had lived all our lives wrapped in cotton wool. Our Berlin apartment was centrally heated, its windows double-glazed and there was hot water constantly on tap. Apparently such technological marvels had not yet reached London. Nor had *bettgewant*, the fluffy down-filled duvets which draped our beds in Berlin. Yet we had never regarded ourselves as privileged. I suppose in our ignorance we imagined that everyone lived as comfortable a life as ours. It was a rude awakening to reality.

We stayed in the Jewish Shelter for two days before returning to Liverpool Street and the north-bound train for Newcastle.

Volunteers from the Refugee Association came to see us off. After that, we were on our own. Paula and I spent the journey inspecting England through critical eyes. The entire landscape was bleached white with frost and the cold seeped into the carriages, making us huddle up in our greatcoats. But we were hugely impressed with the luxury of the train. Even in third class the seats were upholstered, and there were little mirrors in which we admired ourselves.

Siche was there at Newcastle station to greet us. It was a curious greeting, but one that was utterly in character with the brother we had last seen fleeing down the back stairs.

He stood under the window of the compartment, his hand on the door, preventing us from pushing it open.

"Give me your handbags," he demanded.

Paula and I were outraged. Surrender our lovely handbags? Never!

Siche said: "Give me your handbags or I'll not let you off the train."

He meant it. There was nothing we could do. We handed them over with as much ill-grace as we could muster.

"That's better," said Siche, opening the door with one hand and rifling through the bags with the other.

Paula and I exchanged glances as if to say: "He's as bad as he's always been."

We got the bags back later, only minus the hidden £10 notes. Siche, in that irritating big brotherly way of his, had insisted that he look after the money.

He was staying at the Talmudical College but he guided us onto a double-decker bus for the last leg of our journey to Gateshead. From the top deck of this strange bus, we surveyed a bleak and unpromising landscape. Before we had left Berlin, we had pored through our encyclopaedia to find out all we could about the region. So we already knew that Gateshead was in the heart of England's industrial north east. Its chief industries were coal mining, ship building and engineering. But we had no conception what this actually meant in terms of the environment until we saw it before our eyes.

The snow here was different from the crisp white blanket which muffled the countryside we had passed through on our way north. Here it was a dirty grey. Wherever we looked we saw huge chimneys belching out smoke into a sky even greyer than the snow. Occasionally we passed a slag heap, transformed into a mini alp under its coating of grimed snow. We were more than a little depressed.

We clambered down off the bus and set off through never-ending streets in search of our new home. As we approached it our hearts plummetted to our boots. The house was one of fifty or so identical houses in a long skinny terrace. From the outside it appeared too small for any family to live in. I tried not to think about the Agricola Strasse as Siche knocked on the door.

The house, when we stepped inside, was indeed humble. But Mr. and Mrs. Somerfield, our sponsors, were endowed with a wealth of warmth and kindness that cheered us. We could never have guessed it, but we were two very fortunate young ladies to find ourselves under their wing. The Somerfields plied us with solicitous questions. How was the journey? Were we hungry? Did we want to rest? We had only the vaguest grasp of English and they did not speak German but we made ourselves understood in Yiddish.

The Somerfields' daughters, Kylie and Golda, were equally thoughtful to these two usurpers in their family home. The girls were of the same age as us and our friendship was sealed within minutes.

From the moment we stepped through the door until two months later when we left, the entire family seemed dedicated to ensuring that we were happy and comfortable.

Happiness they could manage. Comfort was something altogether different. But that was no fault of theirs. The Somerfields lived a simple existence, a world removed from the cosseting we had always taken for granted.

The first big shock came when I wanted to use the bathroom. Kylie took me out into a tiny back yard and pointed at a wooden door. "There it is," she said.

An outdoor toilet! I thought such things existed only in the *shtetl*.

I grew to hate that toilet, especially in the long dark nights when I lay shivering in bed, too frightened of the dark to venture into the back yard. God knows what might be lurking there. Rats? Mice? Monsters?

I don't think I ever stopped shivering. There was only one source of heat in the house, a boot-black range in the cramped parlour. It had various trap doors in it which served as ovens. There were hot plates on the top and a huge kettle perched on a swivel stand, so that it might be swung over the range when hot water was needed. One of the trapdoors opened to reveal a meagre fire. Its coals glowed and smoke wafted up the chimney, and I suspect most of the heat went up there too. The Somerfields always gave us prime position right in front of its feeble glow. But while the fire warmed my feet, so much so that I soon sprouted a crop of itchy chilblains, somehow my back was always frozen. How I yearned for the great

Kacheloven which warmed me through and through in the Polish *shtetl*.

Bath night every Sunday was another nasty shock. No fewer than 15 kettles were boiled, one after the other, and emptied into a large tin tub placed in front of the fire. I sat in it, my legs scalded red by the hot water, but my skin covered in goosepimples everywhere above the water line.

Paula and I shared a narrow bed, huddling together as February raged outside and an icy wind from the Steppes lashed the north east. Our sole comfort was a brick hot water bottle. If you touched it, you burnt your toes. If you didn't, your feet froze.

Outside, the streets of Gateshead were dreary and uninviting. Night and day the factory chimneys puffed out clouds of smoke that stung your eyes and soiled everything they touched. There was always an acrid tang of soot in the air which pervaded everything. In the back yards grey washing hung from every line.

Yet in the midst of this wasteland lived the kindliest, most cheerful people imaginable. Their ready smiles and open friendliness were strangely at odds with the surroundings. I soon became used to the corner shopkeeper's morning greeting: "All reet, bonnie lass?"

But we were not "all reet." We were permanently frozen to the marrow. Paula and I bemoaned our circumstances privately, for we were anxious not to hurt the Somerfields. We soon came to realise that in volunteering to tend for us this gentle family were making enormous sacrifices which they could ill afford.

So while we may have lacked the luxuries of life, we were constantly showered with affection and care. They cheerfully shared everything they had and did everything humanly possible to make us happy. We could not have found a kinder family anywhere in England. All this we realised.

But that did not stop us writing, in our first letter home, the urgent instruction: "Please <u>IMMEDIATELY</u> send our duvets. We are freezing!"

DIASPORA

When you are a child, you may not quite understand what is happening around you, but you have the innate conviction that sooner or later it will all make sense.

This is how I felt in the early months of 1939 as we waited for Mutti, Papa and Myer to join us. We knew there was some sort of delay but we did not understand what caused it. Someday it would become clear.

It never did. Looking back, almost sixty years on, I can still make no sense of it. For once, the Nazis were not to blame. The only reason I can give for the hold up was British red tape.

This crazed bureaucracy was utterly surreal. It might even have been comic, had it not led to such horrendous tragedy. I have often tried to fathom the rationale behind the Whitehall officials' thinking, but I confess it defies understanding.

Briefly, this was the situation in 1939: Czech Jews were labelled "friendly aliens" by the British, and as such could visit or sometimes even stay in Britain. Provided of course they were able to prove they had jobs for the duration of their stay and would not be a burden on the State. This did not mean they were automatically in line for naturalisation, but at least they had a foot on the bottom rung of a very, very long ladder.

But Jews from Poland, Germany, Austria and almost every Eastern European state were classed as "unfriendly aliens." Their visa applications were subject to rigorous scrutiny by the Home Office. There was more than a touch of raging paranoia among the immigration officers. Any applicant who fell under the unfriendly alien classification was deemed to be a potential Nazi spy, a saboteur, a troublemaker. Time after time Jewish Members of Parliament, rabbis, judges and leading industrialists had to intercede on behalf of these so-called unfriendly aliens to assure the Home Office that a family of would be immigrants were persecuted Jews and not a fanatical Nazi spy cell.

The "unfriendly aliens" were usually those who had already suffered most at the hands of the Nazis. That cut little ice with the British bureaucrats. Nor did the fact that the asylum seekers were often doctors, technicians, scientists, artists, scholars – people who had so very much to offer their new country.

Our grandparents were Polish Jews whose appeals for entry permits gathered dust in the Home Office as the world lurched towards War. Every morning they scanned the mail for the all-important manilla envelope with a stamp bearing the head of King George. It did not come.

Papa was becoming increasingly fearful that the family might not get out in time. He, Mutti and Myer could all emigrate, thanks to their Czech passports. But Mutti was determined to stay until Britain granted permission for Oma and Opa to leave too.

Papa's textile company had ceased functioning because it was no longer safe for a Jew to conduct any business. But Papa was adamant he would not arrive in Britain as a penniless refugee. He was haunted by the memory of the hardship he had suffered when

My maternal grandmother, Rachel Rothenberg, and one of her sons, my Uncle Joseph. Oma Rachel passed away peacefully at her Berlin home during the War. Uncle Joseph escaped to Palestine.

he first arrived in Berlin twenty years before. He was determined his family would not be plunged into the same misery.

And so, as the Nazi net tightened, he dilligently went about collecting money from his various debtors. Friends and couriers smuggled it across the border into Czechoslovakia to join the family nest egg in the Central Bank.

Each new day brought fresh stories of murder and outrage against the Jewish community. Yet still my parents lingered in Berlin, waiting.

Their letters to us gave no hint of the anguish and fear they were experiencing. They even found time to answer our urgent request for our *bettgewant*. And a few weeks later an enormous crate was delivered to the house in Gateshead. Inside it were more warm clothes, a hoard of presents, toys, books, and, most important of all, the lovely fluffy duvets. There was rare jubilation in Gateshead that day.

In their letters Mutti and Papa always sounded cheery and untroubled, and they finished each one with a promise they would join us soon. But an adult's idea of what constitutes "soon" is very different from how a child imagines it.

The days dragged on. In the meantime Oma and Opa had secured the promise of jobs with a Jewish organisation in Britain. That should have been sufficient to win their freedom. But still the Home Office dragged its heels.

Then in March, the family was finally stung into action. Hitler invaded Czechoslovakia. While Britain and the West were bitterly condemning the Nazis' aggression, the Home Office was indulging in another piece of Alice-in-Wonderland bureaucracy. Overnight, Czech Jews lost their privileged "friendly alien" status.

Papa guessed which way the winds were blowing and made immediate plans to leave with Myer and Mutti. But Mutti was intransigent. She agreed that Papa and Myer should get out as soon as possible. She was going to stay on until Britain issued permits for her parents. Papa argued long into the night, but Mutti believed her place was with her increasingly frail parents. In the end, he gave in.

A week or so later, in early April, he and Myer flew into Croydon aerodrome. Air travel was still very much a novelty and Myer was enthralled by it. Papa's mood was tempered by his uncertainty over the reception that awaited them from British authorities.

He was right to be concerned. The immigration officers took one look at their Czech passports and promptly barred them from entering Britain. They were due to be deported back to Berlin on the next flight.

Papa had taken out insurance. A cousin, Bernard Isaak, was waiting for him at Croydon and he promised the officers he would stand as guarantor for Papa and Myer. They still refused.

But a little bit of *Mazel* changed everything. By sheer chance they had arrived on a Friday, before the Shabbos. It was explained to the officials that this was the holiest day of the week for an Orthodox Jew, and to travel after sundown would breach the tenets of his faith. Papa's cousin fetched a respected Rabbi who added his voice to the argument. They must have been very persuasive talkers, for the officials finally relented. But if Papa had arrived at any time other than before the Shabbos, he would have been sent straight back to Berlin.

The officials grudgingly released Papa and Myer into the care of the Rabbi and they were eventually allowed to enter Britain.

There were conditions attached of course. Papa would have to enter a half-way house while his papers were processed. What the officials were saying in effect was that they might still deport him and Myer.

But inwardly Papa's heart was singing. He knew there could be no going back.

Up in Tyneside we were overjoyed at the news of their arrival. In our letters we begged him: "Come and see us, *please.*" Now all we wanted was to have Mutti back and we would be a family again. We pestered Papa with questions: "When is she coming?"

The answer was always the same. Soon.

But it wasn't soon. It was many months before we saw Mutti again.

She stayed in Berlin until the very last moment while Europe trembled on the precipice. Eventually she could wait no longer. Oma and Opa insisted that as a good Jewish wife and mother her place was with her husband and children.

When she went to see them for the last time in their apartment in the Blumen Strasse, it was the saddest of farewells. Mutti still could not shake the sense that somehow she was being disloyal to them in leaving. But Opa was insistent. He told her: "We are old, you are young, Mali. You have to go to your family. You cannot stay another day."

There were similar heartbreaking partings with her brothers and sisters and her many nephews and nieces.

Mutti went back to 21 Agricola Strasse. The big apartment must now have been an empty and lonely place. All there was left was the furniture which she and Papa had chosen over the years. I imagine she went from room to room, casting a last look at the tasselled chairs, the great dining room table, Papa's leather couch, the ornate dressers, the china wedding presents. They would not be needed again, for Mutti had spent some of the long wait ordering an entire new suite of furniture for her future home. It now lay, still in its original packaging, in a dockside storage depot in England, waiting for the day we had a place of our own again. In Berlin, Mutti collected the suitcases which she had packed many months before. She and Bianca hugged each other tightly and then she set off for the station.

She had left her departure until the very last minute. The previous day Hitler's Panzer divisions had rolled into Poland.

Mutti's journey across Germany followed the same path already taken by Siche, Paula and me. The date was September 2, 1939. Her train into Holland was the last one to cross. Three hours after it steamed into Nijmegen the Nazis closed the border. After that there was no escape.

The following morning as Mutti stepped ashore in England, the world was at War.

And, with a terrible irony, that was the morning Opa looked in his mailbox and found the long-awaited letter telling him he and Oma could emigrate to England. But all Germany was a prison camp now.

For a brief period after War was declared there was still a slender line of communication with those who remained in Germany. The Red Cross acted as a form of postal service between the riven families.

There were letters from my aunt Jenni, who still had her splendid apartment in the Charlottenburg. Her husband, Pinkus Fluss, and their two elder children, Sigi and Bertha, were already safe in Britain. Sigi, like Siche, was at a Talmudical college and Bertha, at 16, was working as a domestic drudge. It was a bitter come-down from the luxurious existence she was used to, but at least she was out of harm's way. Aunt Jenni still had her two younger sons and a daughter with her. She tried to keep us all reassured that everyone was well and safe.

We tried to believe her. We read and re-read every letter.

And then the letters ceased.

A long time afterwards we pieced together the various stories as best we could. Oma and Opa had been spared in the Nazi pogroms. They died during the War, but they died in bed. They were given a proper burial and we know their last resting place. That could not be said for most Jews.

Aunt Jenni and her son, Issy, vanished into the camps. There is no way of telling which one. Her daughter, Tosca, and 12-year-old son, Josi, managed to make their way across Germany and into Hungary, where they were put in touch with the great Swedish humanitarian, Raoul Wallenberg. He lodged them in a safe house in Budapest where they were told to stay undercover. They had to live like prisoners. Josi, in happier days, was truly a child prodigy as a violinist. Had he been spared, he would surely have graced concert halls across the world, such was his natural talent. I also remember Josi as a high-spirited boy with a strong streak of independence. He chafed at the restrictions in the safe house. One night he could take no more of this hole-in-the corner existence and he ran into the street. Tosca gave chase but he slipped away in the darkness. He was never seen again. His fate can only be guessed at. Perhaps he was conscripted into forced labour, or into the army on the Russian front, for even children were grist to the Nazi War machine. Or perhaps he was among the one and a half million Jewish children to perish in the camps.

Tosca barely survived and was found after the War in a displaced persons camp in Hungary.

Aunt Ella, who had sheltered Siche after he shot the SS man, escaped to Jamaica with her daughter Jenni. At one stage they were interned there because of their German background. Her eldest daughter, Eva, who was already married, found sanctuary in Portugal. Her other daughters, Sophie and Martha, made it to England. Her youngest sons, Ben and Leslie, came to Gateshead, via the *Kindertransport*. But her three elder boys who had fled to Russia early in 1938 were lost. It is possible they were conscripted into the Red Army and died in the terrible carnage of the Eastern Front. We never heard from them again.

Papa's sister, my aunt Bertha Schutz, managed to get her three daughters out of Berlin. Betty, who was the same age as I, went to Switzerland where at the age of ten she became a maid. The work was hard and unremitting, but at least she escaped.

Her elder sister, Ruth, who was in her late teens, embarked on an astonishing journey, walking through France to Spain and then recrossing the south of France. She eventually walked all the way to Palestine where she settled in a kibbutz near Galilee.

The youngest daughter, Bronya, at only two years old, was smuggled across the border into Belgium. There she joined the ranks of the so-called Hidden Children who were shielded from the Nazis by Gentile families. Bronya was raised by a warm and loving Christian couple and she felt herself so much a part of their family that when the War ended she did not want to return to her mother. But as good Christians, the couple knew they could not keep Bronya, regardless of how much they loved her. They brought her to England and gave her back to her overjoyed mother.

Mutti's nephew, Rafuel Margolis, was the one who established the beachhead in Gateshead. His brother, Leo, was caught in a Nazi round up and sent to Buchenwald. But Leo was determined to survive. In the closing days of the War he realised the Russians were advancing across Germany, and he also knew that the Nazis would do their utmost to kill all the camp's inmates so that there would be no one left to tell the world of their babarism. Leo began making plans for escape. He was detailed to head an outside work unit of six prisoners. Whenever the guards were not looking, he and his group would dig up plant roots and hide them in a forest cache just beyond the camp's perimeter. That part was relatively easy. But the next stage of the plan was much more audacious, and much more fraught with danger. Leo and his comrades built themselves an underground bunker, right under the noses of the patrolling sentries. By now the men in the work unit were little more than scarecrows, and perhaps the guards never suspected there was an ounce of resistance left in them. At any rate, the bunker went undetected.

The sound of the Soviet artillery came closer and closer, until one night Leo and his party slipped out of their hut, and dodging the lights from the machinegun towers, they fled to their underground bolthole. For six days and six nights they huddled there in silence, listening as the camp guards combed the forest for them. Sometimes the searchers came within feet of their lair. Throughout this time the fugitives sustained themselves with their meagre store of provisions.

Gradually the hunt tailed off, and Leo deemed it safe to lead the men through the woods towards the sound of the Russian guns which now seemed only a few miles away. The entire work unit must have presented a sorry sight as they gave themselves up to the Soviet troops. Here, in the middle of a battlefield, were six emaciated figures in filthy and torn striped uniforms, without even a penknife to defend themselves.

Among Leo's comrades was a 17-year-old Rumanian boy, who even at that young age was a veteran of three other camps, Birkenau, Auschwitz and Buna. He was the only survivor of his entire family. His name was Elie Wiesel. Later he was to become a celebrated author and journalist. He wrote of his experiences in the camps and the unit's flight through the forest in his first novel, *Night*.

Mutti's brother Sigi – Aunt Klara's husband – was snared in one of the pre-War dragnets for Polish Jews and sent back to Poland. At first he was safe there but then the Nazis invaded and began their systematic purge. Uncle Sigi was taken and vanished into the camps. We believe he may have perished at Auschwitz.

Mutti's sister, Toni, emigrated to Palestine in the early Thirties. My Uncle Joseph also found refuge in Palestine. Other friends and relatives escaped to China, South America, Canada, the States, Sweden, wherever they could find a safe haven.

Looking back at this Diaspora, there does not appear to be any pattern to it. Why did one member of a family emigrate to Shanghai and another to Caracas? It didn't seem to make any sense.

But there was a considered logic to this scattering of the clans. In 1938 in Berlin, when it became increasingly obvious that flight was the only hope, members of the Jewish community began collecting foreign visas. It was quite a thriving black market. During the week, men would do the rounds of all the embassies in Berlin, picking up whatever permits they could. These visas changed hands on Friday nights in the synagogues, for they were the only places where Jews could conduct business without the risk of eavesdroppers.

Entry permits for America fetched the highest prices, but they were at a premium. British visas too were extremely limited. So people looked elsewhere. The easiest to obtain were those for China, which explains why so many Jews ended up in Shanghai. Their settlement there rapidly expanded and when the War was finally spent, many of the immigrants then made their way to Hong Kong where they played such a vital part in building its economic success. Others from the same far-flung settlement moved on to Canada's west coast.

There were also visas for Palestine, Ireland, Scandanavia, Brazil, Venezuela, Paraguay, Uruguay, and all sorts of unlikely places. One Friday evening at the Adas Synagogue, my uncle Noah, Aunt Ella's husband, bought Jamaican permits for his family. They would eventually mean a passport to freedom for Aunt Ella and Jenni. Papa, for his part, secured six Australian visas. His plan was to emigrate there because it appeared a fresh, untainted land and one filled with opportunity. Mutti, it later turned out, had other ideas. But those visas were essential to the family's entry to Britain, for they showed we were simply passing through.

Other relatives bought whichever visas were available and that is why the family ended up scattered to the far corners of the globe.

Sometimes I leaf through family albums and see all those happy, innocent faces smiling back at me. Here a photograph of a Bar Mitzvah, there one of a family wedding, another of a boisterous birthday party. So many memories spill out of the black and white snapshots.

These were the dear aunts, uncles and cousins who filled my childhood days. For they were more than kith and kin. They were among my closest friends in the world. And we were allowed all too brief a time together.

BACK TO SCHOOL

In England, Paula and I were also on the move. Mr. Somerfield had given up the unequal task of making us feel at home and had sought out new temporary parents. Before we left, he made it clear he was sending us elsewhere for our own comfort. We greeted the news with decidely mixed feelings. On the one hand we really yearned for a home where the windows didn't rattle in the winds and there was warmth. But we also knew we would sorely miss the Somerfields and their all-embracing kindness. What would our new sponsors be like? And there was another concern. For the first time since we had escaped Berlin, Paula and I were to be parted.

Our farewell to the Somerfields was sad and subdued. But we need not have worried about our new homes. Mr. Somerfield had gone to considerable pains to find us the right places with the right people. Paula went to the Galewskys who had three daughters, all older than she.

I was given a home by the Goldbergs who instantly made me feel welcome. They had a tall and very pretty daughter, Rosalind, who was the same age as I, and we shared a warm and airy bedroom with bright flowery wallpaper and its own fireplace. Luxury! There was an elder equally pretty daughter, Edith, and a son, Victor. He was tall and handsome, and shortly afterwards, when he became a junior officer in the Merchant Navy, he cut a dashing figure in his smart uniform.

The Goldbergs' house, although it was terraced, was in a genteel area of Sunderland and it was much more spacious than the Somerfields' modest home. And – joy of joys! – its refinements included an inside lavatory.

Paula's surroundings were altogether more opulent. The Galewskys lived in a large detached house with a big well-kept garden. Next door there lived a little girl called Esther, a refugee from Vienna. She too had been rescued by the *Kindertransport*. Esther soon became our closest friend in England.

Mr. Goldberg owned property, rows and rows of little terraced houses in the back streets of Sunderland. He rented them out for as little as sixpence a week. A sixpence was little more than today's two pence.

Every week I would go round with him as he collected the rents and entered the sums in a thick black ledger. My reward was a big penny, with the king's head on one side and Britannia clutching a trident on the other. As soon as I could, I would change the penny into four farthings – tiny copper coins with a jaunty little wren on them. Next came the tough decision on how to spend them. They would all go on sweets, but the question was which sweets, for the corner shop offered a multitude of choices. My favourites were the long black sticky strings of liquorice, bags of dolly mixtures, little baby pillows and Five Boys chocolate bars.

I had not been at school since early January back in Berlin, and the Goldbergs were anxious to keep up my education, so I enrolled as a pupil in the local elementary school which Rosalind attended. My first impressions of it were not promising. But then my experience was based on the Adas school, one of Berlin's finest.

Paula, on the right, and I coming out of school in Sunderland wearing our prized winter coats.

In Sunderland the classes were much larger, with 40 or more pupils in each. We sat scrunched up on hard wooden seats behind cramped desks while a teacher did his best to keep order. It soon became apparent that education was not a high priority in the area. I was genuinely shocked that many of my classmates could neither read nor write. I suppose the children's future careers were already mapped out. They would leave school at 14 and go straight out to work, the boys as miners and shipyard labourers, the girls as mill workers. All they needed was a very rudimentary education and that is precisely what they got.

School offered me my first taste of English food. I kept solely to a vegetarian diet, largely surviving on baked beans on toast and macaroni cheese. Paula and I were allowed to bring our marvellous coats into class, for the headmaster feared that if we hung them on the hooks in the school cloakroom, they might prove too much of a temptation for a light-fingered fellow pupil.

Thanks to our Berlin schooling, Paula and I rapidly moved up through the classes, so that by the time I was eleven, I was in the top form with the 14-year-olds.

I picked up English fairly rapidly and was soon chattering away with the rest of my classmates. The only snag was I spoke it with the heavy Geordie accent, which is often almost unintelligible to the southern English. It took me several years to shake it off.

I also began Hebrew classes with Rosalind at the *cheder* four times a week and I really enjoyed these sessions. Not, I'm sorry to say, because I was such an enthusiastic student. The real attraction was the social life, for it was at the *cheder* I was able to meet friends from various parts of Sunderland.

Meanwhile Papa and Mutti and Myer were living in London, but making plans to set up home on Tyneside. They were faced with an unexpected problem. The North East was Britain's industrial dynamo and its output was vital to the War effort. Tyneside led the way in building warships, the surrounding coalfields provided the fuel to send them into battle, and a host of factories produced their weaponry and ammunition. This meant that the North East was a restricted area, not open to aliens, friendly or otherwise. As always, the officials who dispensed permission were in no particular hurry to process Papa's request to live there.

The strategic significance of the North East was soon brought home to me for Sunderland became a key target for *Luftwaffe* bombers.

By now I had moved again, for Mrs. Goldberg fell ill and was no longer able to look after me. My new address was 2 Kensington Esplanade, a hostel where there were lots of other Jewish refugees, many of whom had come to England through the *Kindertransport*. We slept six to a room. The hostel was a splendid big Victorian house in a quiet cul-de-sac. It had its own large grounds which gave us plenty of scope to let off our youthful exuberance. Better still, it had proper lavatories and bathrooms. And it was snug.

Another major plus point was its huge cellar which served as an air raid shelter throughout the constant blitz on Sunderland. Every night when we heard the ghostly wail of the sirens, we would troop down to the basement and wait there until the all-clear sounded. The shelter was properly equipped with lights and beds, and sometimes when the bombing went on for hours on end we slept there. I cannot remember feeling afraid. The danger seemed too remote.

But one morning we stumbled out of the basement to find the grey fuselage of a downed German bomber smouldering in our back garden. Even that didn't frighten us. If anything, it made life all the more exciting.

In the summer of 1941 it was decided I had had enough of elementary school. It was time to move up a gear. But there was a problem: it was deemed that my spoken English was fine, but my English writing was not yet strong enough for me to get into the local grammar school, St. Bede's. Instead I enrolled in West Park Central, a girls only school.

Its education facilities were every bit as limited as those in the elementary school. To add to its troubles, many of the teachers had joined the Armed Forces. The system was spartan and I don't know how any of the children were expected to learn anything. Paula had become 14 when she was still at our first school. Her further education was put on hold while she learned shorthand and typing and found herself a secretarial job with a big Jewish firm of furniture makers. Her salary for a 40-hour-week was just half a crown – or little more than 12 pence in today's money. It was certainly not a living wage. However, every Friday night when her boss handed out the pay packets, he secretly gave her another half crown. It was sorely needed and much appreciated.

At school I became the star pupil, for I had inherited Papa's natural ability in mathematics. At one point I scored 100 per cent in the end of term exams. I was of course as pleased as punch. But very soon afterwards I began to wish I hadn't done quite so well. The headmistress called an assembly of the whole school and summoned me up onto the platform to receive a prize. I don't recall what the prize was. All I can remember was the horrible sense of embarrassment I felt as I mounted the steps to the platform, with the eyes of every pupil in the school on me. I stood there, my head down, my face a bright scarlet, as the headmistress heaped lavish praise on me. She then called on all the pupils to applaud. That made things even worse. I dimly remember stumbling back down the steps, my face burning, and desperately wishing I were invisible as all around me clapped and cheered.

But not long afterwards I earned another prize, and one I accepted with a tremendous sense of achievement. It was a cheap whistle. But it was the power it symbolised which gave me such pleasure. It meant I was now in effect the games mistress because the proper teacher was in the Services. I had always been sports crazy and I tackled my new role with relish. I took the girls in the gym for netball and gymnastics. On the sports field I supervised hockey in the winter and rounders in the summer, and that whistle was rarely out of my lips. I am sure my fellow pupils were absolutely sick of the sound of it. But I never tired of its loud "WHEEEP!" nor of the power it conferred.

In 1940 Papa at last won the right to move to Sunderland and it seemed that my long cherished dream of a reunited family was finally coming true. But in those days nothing was ever that simple. The only home Papa could find was the ground floor of a house at 7 Azalea Terrace North and there was not room for all of us – only Papa, Mutti, Myer and Paula. So Siche remained at the Talmudical college and I stayed on in the hostel. But we often took our meals with our parents in the morning room. The dining room was already in service as Mutti and Papa's bedroom.

The Victorian house also had a big front room – the parlour – which was transformed into a bedroom for Paula. There was a very narrow scullery where Mutti did her best to make nourishing meals from wartime rations.

From outside the house might have looked spacious, but our share of it at least was somewhat cramped. The reason for this was that Papa had crammed it with all the smart new furniture he had kept until now in storage. The beautiful dark wood of the huge wardrobes and towering dressers looked strangely out of place in such modest surroundings. Papa used to joke that ours was the best-furnished house in Sunderland, though I'm not sure it was a joke.

Upstairs lived an English couple whose sons were off in the Army. The neighbours were all open and friendly. And despite the meagre rations, the nightly air raids and the devastation of their city, their spirits burned brightly. The Geordies had an unshakeable courage, allied to tremendous good humour. They were easy people to like.

We children had come to take the War in our stride. There were always armed soldiers coming or going, ack-ack batteries on roof tops and the ever-present smell of something burning.

But in the dark winter months of 1940/41 there was a sudden calm. It was as if the whole region had gone into hibernation. The guns fell silent and even the air raids ceased. One look at the frozen countryside told you why. Britain was silent under a blanket of snow and in the grip of an even harsher winter than that of '39. It was so cold that the mighty Junkers and Heinkel bombers were grounded because when they ventured into the frozen skies their wings became iced up and they plummetted to the ground.

Papa was desperately anxious to work, but again the bureaucrats were in no hurry to grant him a labour permit. The inactivity grated on him. He was by nature an energetic man and since almost as far back as he could remember he had worked hard, first helping Oma in the market places and then with his own enterprises. But he still held the Australian visas he had bought years before in the Adas Synagogue. Surely Australia was the place to go? Mutti didn't agree. England was where she wanted to stay. Papa did his best to win her over, pointing out that Australia was warm and sunny, it was safe from the nightly bomber raids, and it was a land of opportunity. Mutti shook her head. She was staying here. Afterwards we all had good reason to be thankful she proved so obstinate. For the ship in which Papa hoped we would sail off to Australia was torpedoed by a U-boat with the loss of everyone on board.

In Sunderland, Papa woke each morning, shaved, dressed himself with care and looked every inch the prosperous businessman he had been back in Berlin. But there was nothing for him to do. I imagine he felt a real loss of identity. He had to find some way to busy himself. He found an unusual outlet for his energies – he took up cookery.

In the kitchen-cum-living room at Azalea Terrace there was a sooty black range with various doors and hot plates. Papa examined this strange contraption with great thought and somehow devised a way to make it work with maximum efficiency. There were very few set meal times in the household, we just ate when we felt hungry. And thanks to Papa there were always pots of stew or hot meals simmering away in the recesses of the range.

But his *piece de resistance* was his baking. How we used to love racing home from school to scent the mouth-watering aroma of his scones and hot cross buns. We buttered them thickly – or as thickly as rationing would permit – and wolfed them down.

Papa's other chief hobby was listening to the radio for news of the War. He also used it to develop his knowledge of English. We would often sit in the morning room, crowded round the radio – or wireless as it was then universally known – and listen to Winston Churchill deliver his magnificent speeches. The wireless had a big round dimly lit dial, with the names of far off stations marked on it. Hilversum, Athlone, Mulhouse – places I had never heard of. They somehow made the wireless a source of romance and adventure.

Mutti had quickly come to terms with her new life. Now there wasn't a Bianca or a maid to look after the daily chores it fell to Mutti to do all the washing and ironing, the cleaning and polishing. Perhaps she and Papa might have been excused if they had bemoaned their reduced circumstances. But I never once recall them complaining. They were too concerned about the fate of those they had left behind in Germany and Poland to feel sorry for themselves.

After Papa and Mutti were some months in Sunderland the English family in the flat upstairs moved out and we took over the entire house. I was delighted, for now we could truly be together. I packed up my things at the hostel and moved into the parlour. It felt wonderful to have my very own bed and furniture again.

Yet there was an unforeseen hazzard to family life in Azalea Terrace. It was a quiet residential area, a long way from the docks and the factories. But that didn't apparently make much difference to the *Luftwaffe* and our particular corner of Sunderland suffered too from their night raids. To add to the perils, our bomb shelter was not the most secure place to hide: it was the "coal hole," the small cellar under the stairs where the coal was kept.

Whenever the sirens sounded we stopped whatever we were doing and we all squeezed in together with only a candle for light.

We sat there, our ears straining for the first distant whine of the heavy bombers as they lumbered towards us through the dark skies. And then came the sounds of their bombs, ripping houses and whole streets apart. We were silent, trying to picture the devastation and death the bombers left in their wake. There would be a brief lull, and then another wave of planes could be heard through the din of the ack-ack batteries. Now the bombs were closer. Sometimes the house shook and we held our breath, waiting and praying.

A long time afterwards came the eerie wail of the all-clear siren. It was safe to venture out again. We emerged from our refuge smeared in coal dust, frightened but alive.

Outside in the street there was utter chaos. In those early raids the *Luftwaffe* had dropped great bundles of incendiary bombs which set the streets ablaze. Sometimes the fires turned night into day and we became used to the sight of firemen silhouetted against the flames as they heroically strove to rescue people from their blazing homes.

As the Blitz progressed, the *Luftwaffe* stepped up their total War tactics and began dropping land mines. The biggest ones which held 1,000-pounds of high explosive were nicknamed Hermanns, after the Nazi's obese Air *Reichsmarschall*, Hermann Goering. When one of these hit a house, its destruction was total. It was as if the house had never existed. After the raids we went out into the devastated streets. Here and there a house in the midst of a terrace had been violently uprooted. The terrace resembled a row of giant's teeth from which several had been brutally plucked.

Elsewhere there were huge gaping craters in the road and pavements carpeted with shards of glass. And amid this wasteland there were the screams of the wounded, the bells of ambulances, the crackle of flames. Air raid wardens in their tin hats tore at the fallen masonry with their bare hands to rescue those entombed in the ruins of what only an hour or so ago had been a family home.

When morning finally came, the entire city of Sunderland seemed to lie smouldering under a thick pall of smoke.

Yet we learned to cope with the night-time terror. It was something everyone had to endure. All these things we became used to, but occasionally the passage of the War threw up an unforgettable image.

I remember with great clarity the day an astonishing rumour ran through the neighbourhood: *the sea was on fire*. This we just had to see. We piled into our outdoor coats and hurried down to the shore. It was no mere rumour. All along the waterfront the sea was ablaze. We stood there transfixed, watching an orange tide of flame lick the shingles on the beach. The water was on fire way out to sea and smoke billowed up into the leaden sky.

Only later did we learn that the coastal defence batteries had feared a German invasion was imminent. To foil the threatened armada, they poured millions of gallons of gasoline into the sea and set it alight.

In the summer of 1942 Papa at last secured his work permit. It was a tremendous day for him, but one tinged with sadness for us. It meant no more hot buttered scones.

He already had a job lined up, as a warehouseman for a Mr. Books, the owner of a sizeable clothing firm. The work entailed stock control and as such was ideally suited to Papa's experience. He very rapidly made himself indispensable, so much so that he – like Paula – found his wages discreetly doubled.

Papa's spirits soared. Once more he had overcome the drawback of being a refugee. He was a man of affairs again.

OUT OF THE FRYING PAN....

By 1943 Papa had acquired a solid reputation in the clothing business. He had also made valuable contacts. It was time to launch his own enterprise. But he felt he needed a better base than Sunderland, so we packed up all the furniture, said goodbye to our friends and moved to London.

Finding a house was not that easy. All building work had ceased because of the War effort, and the havoc wreaked by the *Luftwaffe* made tens of thousands homeless. But somehow Mutti secured the lease on 114 Fitzjohn Avenue, a splendid house in the heart of Hampstead. It was most impressive. Including the sub-basement, there were five floors and far more bedrooms than we needed. Then, as now, Hampstead was a very pleasant place to live. And there was an extra bonus: London was several degrees warmer than the eternal winter of the northeast.

We took to our new home with unconstrained delight. Instead of the drab anonymous streets of Sunderland, Hampstead offered fascinating shops and cosy coffee houses where friends could meet and gossip. Or when the joys of that paled, there were always marvellous walks on the Heath.

Together again. In the garden of their new home in Hampstead, Mutti and Papa pose with their four children.

In moving south, Papa imagined he would be freeing his family from the nightly bombings. Perhaps he assumed that Hampstead was far enough away from the docks and central London to escape the attentions of the Luftwaffe. Besides, only a few minutes walk from Fitzjohn Avenue was Hampstead underground, the deepest Tube station in Britain. Its platforms and steps deep below the North London clay meant we had a super-safe bomb shelter right on our doorstep. It was a shelter we shared with many thousands of people. Paula was always among the first inside, for as soon as the ghostly wails of the warning siren split the air, she was out of the house and racing for the Tube.

Papa was content that he had found us a relatively safe haven. This sense of security did not last more than a few months.

One fine summery morning as we stepped out into the sunshine after another night in the Tube station, we saw on the skyline several approaching planes. They looked smaller than anything we'd ever seen before and there were flames pulsing out of the rear, as if they were on fire. They also made a strange pop-popping sound. We shielded our eyes against the sun and stared at these strange craft.

Quite suddenly the pop-pop ceased, to be followed by a high-pitched whistle, and then, a few moments later, by the most enormous CRUMP!

We had just witnessed the first wave of a new aerial menace. The doodlebugs, or buzz bombs, or to give them their proper names, the V1 rockets.

They were the world's first guided missiles and they were essentially flying bombs, with a tonne of high explosive in the nose cone. Although they were primitive in design, they brought terrible carnage to London. They also caused widespread panic, for they were quite indiscriminate in their choice of target. The Nazis' aim was to cause wholesale terror among the general public.

The doddlebugs, which had a range of only around 150 miles, were fired from mobile launchers in Holland. They did not have the power to strike further afield than the southeast, so if we had stayed on in Sunderland this was one danger we would not have had to face.

But gradually we came to terms with them. You were safe as long as the engine was popping. Once it cut out, you knew you had only a few seconds in which to find somewhere to shelter.

The Air Ministry soon had their measure too. Coastal defence fighters shot down a great many as they streaked across the Channel. Others were snared in huge aerial nets.

And then, just as we were becoming used to the doodlebugs, an even deadlier menace appeared over the horizon: The V2s. Britain was absolutely defenceless against them. There was no warning because they shot through the sky at a mile a second, much faster than the speed of sound. The only way one knew they were there was when an almighty explosion went off.

The V2 was the brainchild of Dr. Wernher von Braun, head of the German Rocket Research Centre at its secret base of Peenemunde on the Baltic Sea. Deep in its underground silos, carved out of the earth by forced labour, he armed 4,000 rockets to rain down on London.

Their design is still to be found today. Every Scud missile, every Saturn space rocket, is modelled on the same principles as those von Braun devised at Peenemunde half a century ago. At the end of the War von Braun was recruited by the Americans to head their space programme.

The deadly storm of V2s was finally halted thanks to RAF bomb raids and the heroism of saboteurs within the base.

But before then we had a couple of uncomfortably close encounters with the rockets. One night we were sleeping in Fitzjohn Avenue – there had been no air raid warning so we felt safe enough – when a V2 exploded nearby. We were literally blown out of our beds and every pane of glass in the house was shattered.

On another occasion a V2 blew up in the centre of High Holborn at lunchtime, bringing unbelievable chaos to the area. At that time I was studying shorthand and typing at Pitman's College in Holborn. Papa, on hearing of the blast, was terrified that I might be among the casualties.

He closed his office in Bishopsgate and went off to look for me. The streets were blocked with debris and fires in the aftermath of the explosion and it took him a long time to walk the two miles to the scene. When he got there he realised the College had not been hit.

Papa breathed a sigh of relief. But that night he made a decision: two close calls was two too many. London wasn't safe anymore.

It was time we moved on.

Our next stop was Manchester, well beyond the range of the V2s. Home there was the ground floor of a comfortable semi on the leafier edges of this northern city. I suppose my lasting memory of those days is one of greyness. Manchester had a well deserved reputation for rain and, when I look back, I still see the streets glistening. But as in Sunderland, the friendliness of the local people more than made up for the shortcomings in the climate.

To be fair, the mood of greyness was enormously amplified by the deprivations of War. Everything was rationed. Petrol, coal, food, clothes, the most basic neccessities. And even if you had the ration coupons, goods were in short supply. Mutti embarked on what seemed a full time career in queuing. As soon as a grocery shop received a new delivery, the whisper went round the neighbourhood and within minutes a long queue of housewives would form, each clutching her precious sepia-toned ration book. Sometimes she might have to stand in the rain for two hours and, if she was lucky, at the end of it she would come away with a pound of apples. Every civilian was allowed just four ounces of meat a week. Eggs no longer came in shells, but in powder which you mixed with water and cooked. If you closed your eyes and imagined very hard, you could just about capture the faintest flavour of eggs. Bread was hard to come by and fresh vegetables were a rare treat.

All of this I could endure without complaint, but there was one aspect of rationing that really grieved me. I have always had a sweet tooth but now, under the strictures of War, the sugar allowance was limited to four ounces a week. One was rationed to a meagre two ounces of chocolate. Two bites, and it was all gone. It was certainly nowhere near enough to satisfy my hunger for sweet things. I was like a drug addict needing a fix. I used to trudge the streets of Manchester, dreaming of chocolate bars, chocolate drops, whole boxes of chocolates wrapped up with gaudy ribbons. Oh, how I craved them. One day, I promised myself, I will have such a feast of chocolate. In the meantime I had to content myself with buying soya flour at Woolworths and making my own marzipan sweets.

Later, in 1946, when the War was over and Europe was picking up the pieces, I finally indulged my craving. I took a ferry to Belgium, which was somehow escaping the hardship of rationing. I had £25 in my handbag, the maximum amount of sterling that could be taken abroad in those days. I went to the casino at Knokke which also had a sideline as a black market currency exchange. The Casino gave me a huge wad of Belgian francs and off I went in search of a confectionery shop, my mouth already watering at the prospect. I bought no less than 100 bars of chocolate, and, as an afterthought, I went to the grocers and filled my case with six dozen eggs. I even treated myself to several pairs of American nylons which were beyond price in Britain. Then I went to the official currency exchange, handed over my surplus Belgian francs and was given back £25 in sterling. It was the bargain of a lifetime.

When I came back through British customs at Dover, my bulging case aroused suspicion. At the time there was a burgeoning trade in diamond smuggling from Antwerp.

"Please open your case," the customs officer instructed.

I threw back the lid and there were rows and rows of chocolate bars. His eyes popped. You could read his thoughts. "Who on earth would want that much chocolate?"

He was also wondering whether illicit diamonds were salted away under the bright wrappers.

I said firmly: "I don't mind if you break every bar once. But not twice. I don't want to be left with lots of little pieces, I won't be able to eat them."

He gave me a steady look, and I think he realised that I was a crazed chocaholic. Perhaps he too had a sweet tooth. At any rate, he chalked a big white cross on my suitcase and let me through without breaking open a single bar.

But that was later. Back in Manchester in 1945 there was a daily battle to secure life's essentials. There was no time for luxuries. Clothes rationing was severe. A pair of nylons had to last a year. Fortunately those early nylons were made of much sterner stuff than the silky sheer creations of today, and, with considerable darning and patching up, one could just about make a pair last a long time.

We were more fortunate than most in that both Papa and now Siche were deeply embroiled in the textiles industry and so we were able to dress fashionably, despite the privations. Siche had launched his own career in piece goods, that is buying and selling bolts of cloth. But these bore no resemblance to the multi-coloured and patterned materials of today. Everything was made for the utility market. The materials were known as "greys," because they were off-white and had yet to be fully processed.

It required a great deal of imagination and considerable effort to turn these unprepossessing lengths of dull cloth into anything attractive. Paula and I pored over fashion magazines and the showbiz gossip journals to see what the stars of Hollywood were wearing this season. After that we had the material dyed to whichever colours took our fancy and then found a local tailor to cut it into a reasonable approximation of the styles we had chosen.

Attractive clothes were important to me because I now had a job of sorts and had to look my best. I had become a travelling saleswoman, selling various products made by Papa's firm. Every morning I would load a big bag to the brim with zip fasteners, sewing cottons and the various trimmings used by clothes manufacturers. There was also hard, shiny toilet paper, which, believe it or not, was a luxury item. A cousin made batteries, not very good batteries, I'm afraid, and I always added a dozen or so of these to my wares.

I then took a bus to Manchester Piccadilly where there were regular services to all the outlying mill towns. One day Bolton, the next Bradford, or Wigan or Warrington or Eccles or Rochdale or Oldham. I soon got to know the dreary towns where every street seemed to be an outrageously steep hill and where each prospective customer seemed to be at the very top of the hill.

It was hard work, but I enjoyed it. I was also very proud of what I was doing. After all, this is how Papa had begun his business career. This was how his mother, my Oma Rachel, had worked before him.

There was however one aspect of which I was not terribly proud: my cousin's dreadful batteries. At that stage batteries were extremely hard to come by, so when I offered some to a retailer, he was often prepared to buy everything I had – zip fasteners, cottons, the lot – just so that he could have the batteries.

I brought along a torch to demonstrate them in operation. I switched it on, and presto, the bulb lit. So far so good. But the problem was that if I switched it off I could never switch it on again because the batteries for some unfathomable reason worked only once. In my defence, I can only say that I warned the retailers about this rather important drawback. They were not dismayed. They still flocked to buy my wonky batteries because they knew they could sell them on to unsuspecting customers.

Often I was able to dispose of all my wares in my first call of the day. The temptation then was to return home and stock up again. But it was a temptation I resisted. I had a strange superstition that one load was enough. Two was tempting fate. And anyway, I was making quite a lot of money in my progress through the mill towns.

We were in Manchester for around three months before Papa deemed it safe to return to London for the threat of the V2s was now eliminated. So back we went to Fitzjohn Avenue. We found London an infinitely safer city than the one we had left a few short months before. The air raid sirens were all but stilled. In Germany the *Luftwaffe* were too busy fighting off the great 1,000-bomber raids to be able to keep up the Blitz on England. There was a new-found mood among the people. It was no longer a question of "If we win." Now it was "When we win." We were counting off the days and life was returning to some sort of normality.

I had been forced to cut short my secretarial classes at the Pitman Institute and now they no longer appealed to me, for a new career had suddenly presented itself. On my daily rounds of the northern mills I had seen industrial chemists working in the lab of a major elastics company, seeking to improve their products. The factory manager, sensing my interest, offered me a job there. It struck me as a fascinating occupation and I entertained visions of myself in a crisp white coat analysing chemicals in a clean, well-ordered lab. But first I needed the academic qualifications.

I enrolled at University College, part of the London University, on a three-year pharmacy degree. I was just 16 years old and thirsty for knowledge.

The work was intense and there was no allowance made for my shortcomings in English, but I was fortunate in having a boyfriend who steered me through the difficult patches. To be honest, he did most of my homework and even set up experiments for me. He is still a dear friend. With his help I rapidly progressed and found myself in the A stream of students.

I often wonder how my whole life might have been altered had I stuck with my studies. But there was one element of chemistry that no one had seen fit to warn me about: the smell. I truly could not stomach that. Each morning as I approached the lab my nostrils twitched at the stench. It was a nauseous mix of formaldehyde and gentian violet. It didn't seem to bother my fellow students, but it made my stomach perform somersaults. The prospect of a life amid such foul smells was too much. With reluctance, tempered by considerable relief, I left.

A TIME TO DANCE

Throughout the spring of 1945 we were slaves to the radio and the newspapers. Every reported development in the War was hungrily digested and debated and argued over. All over London, families consulted their atlases and charted the Allies' progress along the spine of Italy, across France, through Holland towards the Rhine. There was a constant frisson in the air. We all knew the tide had turned. Three years earlier Churchill had hailed the defeat of the Afrika Korps at El Alamein as "The end of the beginning." In June 1944 the Allies had stormed ashore in Normandy – the beginning of the end. Now we waited for the end.

Yet our new sense of security awakened deeper and darker fears. Released from worries about our own safety, we turned to brooding about the fate of our many friends and relations still trapped in Hitler's Fortress Europe. Our mood veered wildly between despair and hope. There were already terrible stories about the wholesale slaughter of our people. Some of the refugees in London felt it wiser to fear the worst. Others clung desperately to hope, holding it before them like a candle in the storm. They held on until there was no hope left.

It was around this time that I began to notice the change in Papa. It was as if he had lost his marvellous *joie de vivre*. I had seen him smile through those terrible nights in Sunderland when it seemed as if at any moment the house would fall down about our ears. I had clung to him for reassurance when the rockets brought terror to London. All that time his eyes had never lost their sparkle, his conviction that everything would be all right was an invisible shield.

Now that he was no longer fearful for his children's safety, he worried about those he had left behind. For the first time I can remember he seemed vulnerable and withdrawn.

It was a foreboding we could not share, for children are by nature optimists. Then at one minute past midnight on May 8, 1945, Germany surrendered. It was VE Day – the moment when our pent-up anxieties and terrors of the past six years were at last exorcised.

Overnight London became a city of carnivals, where no-one was a stranger. We had all suffered together and now we celebrated together with the most joyous effusion imaginable. The city was filled with soldiers, sailors and airmen from every outpost of the British Empire and from the lands of its allies.

Paula and I and a group of friends boarded the Tube and set off for the Paramount, a dance hall in Tottenham Court Road. When we arrived we found ourselves caught up in a multitude of people, dancing and singing under flags and bunting. It was as if everyone's birthday had come at once.

The packed roadway was a babel of voices – here the laconic drawl of a farm boy from Wyoming, there the guttural tones of a South African, and there the rapid fire chatter of a turbanned Sikh soldier. It was a party for the world, or the free world anyway.

And everyone wanted to dance. Heaven only knows how many partners I had that day. Their conversation was not memorable, mainly because so many of them had only the slightest grasp of English. Nor was their dancing particularly elegant. It largely consisted of a few heady whirls and then I was off on the arm of another partner. Sometimes I danced with a borrowed sailor's cap perched on my head, sometimes wearing the khaki tin helmet of a Tommy.

Above the whirling throng, loudspeakers kept up a running commentary on the latest reports in from Germany. Each new announcement of the Allies taking command of another German town was greeted by heady cheers.

Paula and I danced all day in the street and almost all through the night in the Paramount. From that exuberant helter skelter of celebration it is hard to pluck out a single image. I cannot even recall if the day was sunny, but it certainly seemed so. Nor do I remember whether we ate, the music the band played, the clothes I was wearing. But what I do remember vividly is the smile on everyone's face. We had come through the most awful chapter in the history of the world. We had a lot to smile about. We did not think about the future, for everyone knew that whatever came next could only be better.

But much later, when we went home to Fitzjohn Avenue, footsore and with our heads spinning, Papa wasn't smiling. Our long absence had caused him not a little anxiety. We went off to bed, deeply repentant, but I'm sure as we drifted off to sleep we were still smiling.

Many years later I read of Wellington's bleak comment after he routed Napoleon at the Battle of Waterloo:

"Nothing except a battle won can be half so melancholy as a battle lost."

Never was this more true than in the Allies' victory over Nazism. In the wake of triumph flowed a terrible tragedy. One by one the camps were taken – Belsen, Auschwitz, Dachau, Theresienstadt, Ravensbruck, the endless list. It was only then that the true enormity of what the Nazis had done was revealed to a world appalled. In the cinemas the news reels depicted scenes beyond our worst imagined horrors. After the peace came the grief.

Papa was deeply traumatised. Before the horror he had an enormous zest for life. When his day's work was done, he loved to go out with Mutti and friends. He was an ebullient party host, delighting in filling the apartment with his many acquaintances. Now he had ceased to care, and away from his work he became almost a recluse.

Papa was in effect stricken with guilt, that he and his immediate family had survived, while so many of his friends and their children had perished in the camps. His trauma was quite common among the survivors of his generation but of course in those days the syndrome had not yet been diagnosed.

Mutti and the rest of us tried to ease him out of his depression. It was no use. The despair seemed rooted in his soul. Apart from his work, his one burning interest was in trying to track down those he had lost. All over western Europe and deep behind the Iron Curtain there were displaced persons camps where the skeletal survivors of the death camps were slowly piecing their lives back together and waiting for their loved ones to find them. There were millions of such people. The task of finding one or two or even ten among such a fragmented multitude was awesome. It was left to the various aid agencies to supply lists of survivors.

Papa would spend hours searching through the myriad columns of names. Occasionally a name would leap out which would give him cause to hope, but subsequent checking would cruelly dash it. His search went on for several years after the War had ended.

Only one survived the camps, my cousin Leo Margolis, who had led the escape from Buchenwald. He eventually made it to London in 1946 and we laid on a joyous reunion. We were justifiably proud of Leo, and relatives flocked from all over Britain to welcome him. Of course, it was impossible for any of us to imagine even the tiniest fraction of the horrors he had seen, the brutality he had endured. Our mood was one of utter happiness. But Leo, I recall, was very subdued. He never once spoke of his experiences in Buchenwald, but he patiently told and retold the story of his escape.

Many Jews who had survived the camps lost their faith. They felt perhaps that the God of their fathers had failed them, and they returned with their body, their spirit and their belief shattered. But, if anything, Leo's faith was strengthened by his ordeal. Later, when he emigrated to the States and married, he ensured that his three sons were raised as Orthodox Jews. They were schooled to become successful professionals, but equally important, all three were noted Talmudic scholars.

In London, Papa finally came to accept that Leo was the only one to survive the camps. The others were all lost. This acceptance did not give him any peace. He was still filled with guilt and remorse. "I should have done more," he would berate himself. It was useless Mutti pointing out there was nothing he could have done, for no-one could have forseen Hitler's determination to exterminate every Jew caught in the Nazis' iron fist. Papa retreated inside himself, haunted by memories of that lost generation. It was, I suppose, fitting that his appetite for life should be restored by a new generation. In 1950 he was presented with his first grandchild, Siche's son, Josi. For the first time in many unhappy years Papa

*A single photograph illustrates the family diaspora. Aunt Ella, second from
left, middle row, escaped to Jamaica. To her left, her daughter Eva found
refuge in Portugal, where the twins, Ruth and Naomi (front), were born.
Alongside Eva, my cousin Jenni who briefly settled in Cuba. Her brothers,
Lesley and Ben (back row), came to Britain as child refugees.
On the far left is Leo who led a daring escape from Buchenwald.*

smiled a smile from the heart. Josi's birth represented Papa's
rebirth.

In the wake of the War, Paula and I were learning to explore and
enjoy our new city, for it went without saying that we could never
again live in Berlin.

The only place to be seen was Swiss Cottage, happily just a short
Tube journey from Hampstead. It offered a score of basement cafes

where there were always old friends to be found, and new friendships to be made. We went there every night of the week, dressed in our smartest clothes, for, quite apart from anything else, Swiss Cottage was also the hub of the universe for all the local boys.

The cafes had the same utilitarian look as anywhere else in the capital. Hard wooden benches lined the walls, candles augmented the feeble glow from 40-watt bulbs, and where there were tables they were more likely than not old orange boxes. Often the most potent beverage on offer was a glass of lemon tea. Luxury it wasn't.

But the spirited atmosphere of the cafes more than made up for their other deficiencies. The ambience was bohemian, long before Soho caught on to the trend. Here every night an astonishing cavalcade of singers, poets, musicians and actors stood up on makeshift stages and performed their party pieces for our enjoyment. It was in such a cafe that I first saw the young Theodore Bikel who went on to be a celebrated character actor in films. Musicians who were later to become household names performed there too, sometimes in exchange for a glass of lemonade, or, if they were lucky, a glass of wine.

It was not until the Sixties that they coined the term Swinging London. Young people then had the bright spots of Chelsea as their haunts, and I'm sure they had a wonderful time of it. But I'm equally sure that our Swiss Cottage days were even more enjoyable, for our generation was emerging from its own dark age, and we dedicated our every spare moment to enjoying ourselves. Despite our wartime experiences – and there were many refugees among our wealth of friends – there was also a sweet innocence about that period. Drugs were unheard of, sex had not been invented. But above all there was the sheer joy of being alive, being there.

Whenever I look back upon those Swiss Cottage days, I find myself smiling with fond memory.

Of course life was not simply a hectic round of pleasure-seeking. One had to work too. I had made a dramatic switch of careers and was now articled to an accountant. The head for figures I had inherited from Papa was beginning to pay dividends.

Social life too had its responsibilities. It was very popular among girls to join or form charity committees. I got myself onto the Three C's, a rather upmarket charity group.

It was in my guise as a committee member that I approached an old friend from Berlin, Simon Reiss, whose father used to play cards with Papa all those years ago in Agricola Strasse. I sold Simon and his young wife, Trudie, tickets to the Three C's gala ball in Claridge's, the most prestigious venue in London.

Simon said: "Make it three tickets. I want to bring a friend along."

This friend, he explained, had just recently returned from active service in India and was now in charge of a prisoner-of-war camp in England.

I thought no more about it. On the night of the ball I dressed with special care for I was one of the organisers and I knew I had to do a lot of mingling. I wore a long black dress in silk jersey with a sweetheart neckline – the very epitome of fashion then. The dress was beautifully cut and made me ever so slender. I tried it on in front of my bedroom mirror and was awfully pleased with myself. I also wore black shoes with platform heels and ankle straps. I had had to send off for the shoes, for if you didn't have platform heels and ankle straps you just weren't part of the scene.

My boyfriend, Johnny, another veteran of the *Kindertransport*, was a well-to-do jeweller. I say boyfriend, but he was really more a friend.

It was Christmastime 1948, and London was doing its best to emerge from the drab shadows of the post-War gloom. We set off for Claridge's in a mood of high excitement. But as soon as we entered the magnificent ballroom I had to wave my escort goodbye, for I was supposed to mix with the other guests.

I threaded my way from one group to another until Simon Reiss called me over. He and Trudie were with a tall, personable man whom I had not seen before. He might have been a stranger in town, but he was very much at ease. He had blue amused eyes which looked at me directly.

Simon said: "Susi, I'd like you to meet Freddie."

"I've heard quite a lot about you already," he said with a smile. His voice was soft and well spoken. There was an air of the gentleman about him. We shook hands and I turned my attention to Trudie, admiring her dress and asking her if she was enjoying the ball. Yet all the while I could feel the stranger's eyes on me. Naturally I felt flattered by the gaze of such an attractive man.

When Simon and Trudie went off to dance we were left together. I attempted to make polite conversation but he stopped me dead in my tracks by saying: "My name is Freddie Breitfeld. I want you to remember the name because it is going to mean something to you."

This was said not in a boastful way but as a plain statement of fact. I looked up into his eyes. There was a twinkle of humour in them, but his voice was deadly earnest.

I'm not at all sure how I reacted outwardly. Inwardly I was quite rocked on my heels. And I regret to say that I totally neglected my mingling duties for the evening, preferring to dance and talk to my new-found companion. In my defence, all I can say is he was such fascinating company. There were in the ballroom several hundred young women from the upper reaches of London's Jewish society. Some of them were very beautiful indeed. Yet he made me feel as if I were the only woman in the room.

At the end of the ball, Johnny found me again and took me home, but not before Freddie had taken a note of my phone number.

I think I had more than a little difficulty getting to sleep that night. In the morning I was still snuggled up in bed when the phone rang.

Paula called upstairs: "Susi, it's for you."

I called back down: "Who is it?"

From Paula: "I don't know. He says his name is Freddie."

I was out of bed and into my dressing gown in a split second. Any pretence I might have had about being a demure young lady vanished as I took the stairs two at a time.

"Hello?" I said breathlessly down the phone.

And at the other end came the brown handsome voice of the night before.

Two weeks later we were engaged.

A PERFECT MATCH

When it came to planning for his children's futures, Papa was the most cautious of parents. Particularly where his daughters were concerned.

And especially when I was involved.

He and Mutti regarded me – with some justification – as headstrong, impulsive and a shade unpredictable. So later that night when I broke the news that I had met the cleverest, most handsome, most charming man in the world, Papa frowned. Mutti froze in what she was doing and just stared at me.

"Who is he?" Papa demanded.

Pink-cheeked and still a trifle breathless after another night's dancing, I spilled it out in one quick-fire sentence.

"His name is Freddie – Freddie Breitfeld. Yes, Papa, he's from a good Jewish family. He was a soldier, a staff sergeant-major and he's –"

"Breitfeld?" Papa cut in. "I don't know any Breitfeld."

Mutti, ever the peacemaker, said quickly: "You must invite him home so that we can see him."

"He's coming tomorrow evening," I said, for I was every bit as keen that Freddie should meet Mutti and Papa.

Freddie's pride and joy was his gleaming Studebaker saloon. I was less enraptured with the car. Every journey seemed to end up with me helping him push it.

I can honestly say that I did not have the faintest flicker of concern over the impending meeting. I was utterly convinced that my parents too would fall under Freddie's spell.

I had always brought my boyfriends home and Mutti and Papa had always made them feel welcome. But I had never been in love before. I knew that this time Papa was planning to subject Freddie to a barrage of questions to determine if this man was suitable for his wilful daughter. I wasn't concerned. After all, how could Papa find anything wrong with someone so perfect?

I made the introductions and then slipped off to the kitchen with Mutti, leaving Papa and Freddie to have their man-to-man talk in the drawing room. The time ticked by and I began to get a trifle impatient. I didn't want Papa monopolising my beau for the entire evening.

Mutti counselled: "Be patient. They have much to talk about."

I said: "Isn't he wonderful, Mutti?"

She said: "He is a real gentleman, Susi." A real gentleman was Mutti's highest form of praise.

Eventually the drawing-room door opened and Freddie and Papa came out together. They were both smiling and it was immediately apparent that they had forged a bond of friendship. I fetched my coat and my handbag, anxious to go off and enjoy the rest of the evening in Freddie's company. But it took me a good hour to prise him and Papa apart. Every time I thought I had succeeded, one of them would launch into a new topic and the conversation would start all over again. It was as if each struck sparks off the other.

That introduction set the pattern for a lifelong friendship. Papa could never look upon Freddie as merely a suitable son-in-law. In truth, he bestowed upon him as much love and affection as he showered on his own sons. It was a love which Freddie reciprocated. Mutti too was an ardent admirer. Her dark eyes lit with laughter and pleasure every time he came calling for me.

So in the space of just a few hours Mutti and Papa were both firmly convinced that the young man I had met only a couple of days ago was the ideal husband for their younger daughter.

After that it was my turn to meet Freddie's parents, and this time I did have a certain trepidation. I so much wanted them to approve of me. But any trace of nervousness vanished within moments. They took me to their hearts, just as Mutti and Papa had done with their son. It was a wonderful moment. I felt as if I had known them all my life. And I soon understood where Freddie had inherited his manners, his charm and his intelligence.

Herman and Resi Breitfeld had the same values, the same qualities as my own Mutti and Papa, so it came as no surprise that the two sets of parents hit it off from the very start. It was a warm and easy friendship that lasted all their days. Even if Freddie and I had not married, I feel sure the parents would have remained close friends.

We wanted to marry as quickly as possible. But Papa's innate caution resurfaced. He said: "That's all very well. But you can't get married until you find somewhere to live. When you find a place of your own, then we can talk about your getting married."

Nowadays that would not pose the slightest problem. One would simply do the rounds of the estate agents and take one's pick of the properties up for sale. The only difficulty now would be choosing exactly which home from the hundreds on offer.

But this was the winter of 1948-9, when all across Britain tens of thousands of houses and apartment blocks had been reduced to rubble by the Blitz. And because of the labour shortage, few new homes were being built.

Papa was most anxious that we choose a house, and the bigger the better. Now it was my turn to dig my heels in. "A house!" I wailed. "I don't want a house. I've never had a broom in my hand, I've never made a pot of tea. If I had a house I would spend all my time just looking after it. All I want is a little flat."

"You don't want a flat," Papa argued. "A house is better. And it is easier to find a house than a flat."

That was true, but I still was absolutely determined that our first home would be a manageable flat which did not entail too much scrubbing and dusting.

Papa shrugged. "All right. You want a flat. But remember, you don't get married until you find one."

I chafed at Papa's restriction but I saw the wisdom of it. Freddie was typically practical about it. "Let's start looking," he said. And soon we were combing the streets of North London for To Let signs.

In the intervening months I got to know a great deal about Freddie Breitfeld. And there was a great deal to know. Like me, he came from an Orthodox background. His family, originally from Hungary, had settled in Vienna where, before the War, they had a prestigious fur business. That, of course, had since been appropriated and looted by the Nazis, in much the same way that Papa's Berlin enterprise had been stolen from him.

Freddie went to high school in Vienna and later to the celebrated *Handelsakademie* business school where he also learned English. Besides Freddie, there were two other sons, Ernest and Paul, who were several years younger.

The boys' father, Herman Breitfeld, was a man with a cool intelligence. As early as 1938 he foresaw that Austria too would turn on its helpless Jewish community. He moved the family to Switzerland and the following year to England.

Freddie was the first to arrive. He stepped off the train at Liverpool Street, hailed a taxi, and in his best English gave the driver directions. The words were all right, but his pronunciation made them gobbledygook. The cabbie looked at him sorrowfully and said: "Tell me again in Yiddish. Yiddish I understand."

It was a shaky start, but Freddie soon found his feet. Ever keen to learn, he took an economics degree at London University and in the evenings studied at St. Martin's School of Art. It was there that he developed a passion for architecture and all his life he remained a frustrated architect. I am quite sure that if he had not devoted his creative drive to building up his business enterprises, he would have been quite happily engaged in designing buildings.

The youthful Freddie Breitfield shortly after his arrival in England.

In 1940 he was plucked from the family business and conscripted to serve in an anti-aircraft battery, defending London against the nightly *Luftwaffe* raids. His post was on Hampstead Heath, less than a mile from our home. Sometimes I would see the Army trucks rattle past with their cargo of khaki-clad soldiers on their way to man the ack-ack guns. But I never dreamed that my future husband might be among those men.

After a few months on the battery – and without much success in shooting down bombers – Freddie was transferred to the Volunteer Corps, whose ranks were largely made up of similar "friendly aliens." He found himself serving alongside old friends.

The Army's original plan was to send Freddie to the Far East on active service, but that idea was scuppered when during his medical examination the doctors found traces of an old injury. When he was just a little boy, Freddie was nearly killed in a car accident. The injury had left a lasting scar which made it impossible for him to wear the tin battledress helmet. And that in turn meant he could not be drafted for active service.

But the Army deemed he was too valuable a conscript to lose, so they gave him a desk job in administration. He was horrified to find that many of his colleagues lacked even the ability to read and write. And he was certainly over-qualified for the routine paperwork assigned to him. Before long it became obvious to his senior officers that they were wasting a valuable asset, for Freddie had a natural aptitude for administration. He even had an economics degree and a diploma in business studies to prove it.

So he was rapidly promoted. But once again the top brass felt he had a more important role to play and along came another promotion. And another. Until he caught the eye of the First Sea Lord and Commander-in-Chief of South East Asia, Lord Louis

Mountbatten. He promptly stole the young Austrian Jew to serve on his Brigade Staff with the Allied Liberation Force, South East Asia.

As a staff sergeant-major, the highest rank a non-commissioned officer can attain, Freddie went with Mountbatten to Java, Ceylon, Burma, Singapore, India and all over the Asian theatre of operations. Mountbatten was so impressed with his diligence and cool efficiency that he recommended him for an OBE. Sadly, the honour was denied Freddie because he was not a naturalised British subject. There is a grim irony that many of the Jewish conscripts were judged suitable to fight and even die for their adopted country, but were disbarred from receiving its honours. Though whenever Freddie related the story of his lost OBE, he always told it with much rueful laughter and never the slightest trace of bitterness.

Mountbatten esteemed him so highly that when Singapore was finally retaken from the Japanese, he made Freddie the military mayor over its two million people. It was a huge responsibility for one so young – he was only in his mid-twenties – but Freddie took up the gauntlet with enthusiasm, as Mountbatten knew he would. Between his crowded hours re-establishing a proper civilian administration for Singapore, he even found time to tend to the pastoral welfare of the men under him. Freddie was particularly keen that the Jewish boys in the Army in Asia be allowed to observe the rites and ceremonies of their faith. Through his closeness to Mountbatten he was able to ensure they received leave on special occasions and on the high holy days. He also made sure their dietary needs were met.

His final service posting was as governor of a prisoner-of-war camp in the Home Counties. He had been demobbed only a brief time before we met that night at Claridge's. Now he was eager to restore the family's fur trade to its pre-War eminence. This was more than just a business. It was part of a proud family tradition which involved many Breitfelds in various countries in Central Europe.

Among them was Freddie's uncle, Marcel, who was responsible for one of the most astonishing Jewish rescue operations in the entire course of the War.

Before the Nazis installed a puppet government in Budapest, Marcel Breitfeld was one of the Hungarian elite. If not an aristocrat by birth, he was certainly regarded as such. His magnificent mansion, his generosity, his sumptious parties were legendary in Budapest. A gilt-edged invitation to a Breitfeld gala ball was proof that the guest had reached the social pinnacle.

Naturally, with the unopposed Nazi invasion of Hungary, Marcel Breitfeld adopted a lower profile. But he remained on the best of terms with the city's nobility. And it was through his contacts with them that his dream of the great escape was realised.

The year was 1943, when Hitler's once all-conquering War machine had begun to suffer its first serious reverses. His divisions had been rebuffed on the eastern front, denying him the prized Ukrainian oilfields. In Africa too, the defeat of Rommel frustrated Hitler's plan to seize the massive refineries in the Gulf. In short, the War machine was rapidly running out of fuel and the Nazis lacked the hard currency to buy supplies.

It was at that moment that Marcel Breitfeld put forward his audacious plan: he would give the Germans a million dollars if they promised safe passage to a freedom train, filled with 400 Jewish refugees. The delicate negotiations, conducted by friendly go-betweens, dragged on, and then quite suddenly the Nazis agreed.

A closed train was provided in a siding at Budapest station. It waited there under armed guard for 24 hours while Marcel gathered together all of his family and close friends and saw them safely aboard. It was a huge undertaking because many of his relatives were unwilling conscripts in the Nazi's eastern front divisions. As part of his extraordinary agreement, Marcel insisted they had to be released.

After his own people were on the train, there were still hundreds of empty seats. Marcel felt he could not possibly decide on who should fill them, for truly, this was a life or death decision. Instead, he asked the leaders of the Jewish community to nominate the other passengers. Sadly, their choice of who should escape created a bitter controversy. For among their nominees were a great many rabbis. Many people argued that the chance of freedom should have been given to the children. Marcel, who would have preferred to rescue the young, was powerless, and the passenger list remained as directed by the community elders.

As soon as every seat had been filled, the sealed train pulled out of Budapest and headed north. It rolled unhindered across the borders of Czechoslovakia, on into Germany and right through to the Baltic where a ferry awaited to bear the 400 refugees to sanctuary in Sweden. It is quite terrible to think that as the express headed towards liberty, all across occupied Europe other sealed trains filled with Jews were rolling towards their awful destinations.

In Stockholm, Marcel set about rebuilding his lost empire. Fur was not as plentiful in Scandinavia as it had been in pre-War Hungary, so he cast around for an alternative. He found the answer in sheepskin. Marcel Breitfeld was the man who gave the world the sheepskin coat. From its modest beginnings with only a handful of workers in Stockholm, his company was soon turning out thousands of fleecy coats which were snapped up by the Swedes. The rest of the world was not far behind. And by the early fifties, Marcel's empire was if anything greater than ever before.

I have a small personal postscript to this story. Many years earlier, when Marcel married, part of his wife's wedding dowry was a magnificent damask table cloth, beautifully decorated with elaborate embroidery. In Budapest it was always laid on the Breitfeld dining table for special occasions. When the family fled Hungary, the tablecloth went with them.

Some years later one of Marcel's daughters gave me this lovely heirloom. Now, on Jewish holidays, it graces my dining table. When the meal is over, we sit around the table, our fingers tracing the intricate hand-stitching and we tell stories about our family. For the cloth is truly the fabric of our history.

We return to 1949 and those frantic months when Freddie and I scoured London for a home of our own. It seemed a hopeless search, but we had not counted on the Jewish bush telegraph. Freddie's father, however, always had his ear attuned to what was going on and he got to hear of a woman friend from Vienna who was planning to move from her flat. Before it could go on the open market, he persuaded her to let us have first refusal.

The flat, in Willesden Lane, was more than we had ever hoped for. It was in a new block, completed only a few months before War broke out. Freddie and I took one look at it and knew this was the place for us. It had a spacious lounge leading on to a dining room. The kitchen was filled with all the mod cons of the day. There were two bedrooms. And the entire flat had been well cared for. And, every bit as important to me, it looked as if it required the minimum of scrubbing and cleaning. We instantly agreed to its rent and to pay key money, as was the custom of the day.

Now Freddie and I were able to set a date for our wedding. We chose August, because that gave us plenty of time to contact all our many friends and relatives. It also gave me a breathing space to do my bridal shopping. Top of the list was my wedding dress.

But here I ran into a stumbling block, and one that not even Papa's nor Mr. Breitfeld's vast network of contacts could help me surmount. Rationing governed everything, and even if I had all the necessary coupons for material, there was little the shops had to offer. The bolts of cloth in the windows all carried the same drab utility look of the day. Certainly, there was nothing on sale that could even remotely be fashioned into a stunning bridal gown, and I had my heart set on looking my absolute best for the big day.

So another search was launched. It seemed that all my spare time – not to mention that of my friends – was devoted to the hunt. We trawled the once-elegant shops of the West End. I pass these same shops now and I see mannequins clad in the latest fashions from Mizrahi, Versace, Lagerfeld, Calvin Klein. But back in 1949, the models sported sombre black suits and utilitarian dresses in an unflattering shade of beige.

But I refused to give up hope. Then I met a sympathetic sales girl in Swan and Edgar's in Regent Street. I was getting desperate by now. I resorted to out-and-out bribery, promising her: "If you can find me something wonderful, I will give you a special present."

She promised she would do her best. A couple of weeks later, the phone rang in our Hampstead house. "I think I've got it," the sales girl reported.

I caught the first Tube down to Oxford Street to be sure I got to Swan and Edgar's before any other customer could snap it up. The sales girl greeted me with a triumphant smile. "I think you'll like this."

And from under the counter she produced a bolt of silver brocade.

I was speechless. If it had been made of spun gold I don't think I could have been more astonished. I held the ever-so-beautiful material up against me and little sparkles of light danced as it moved. I had never seen anything so elegant. It was utterly perfect.

"I'll take it," I said, without even asking the price.

There were only four yards of the silver brocade. It would take someone special to fashion this small piece of material into a wedding dress. Fortunately I knew such a marvel. A very good friend of mine was a couturier in the fashion house of Norman Hartnell, who later became the Queen's favourite designer. She took the brocade and turned it into a breathtaking bridal gown. It had a slim figure-hugging bodice, long sleeves and a ruched skirt. There was not of course enough material for a bridal train, but it did not need one. When I tried on my dress for the first time, I felt like a princess. Mutti, Paula and my friends oohed and aahed over it. I couldn't wait for the 25th of August when Freddie would see me in it.

The build-up to the wedding was conducted in the Orthodox tradition, which required that for the week prior to the ceremony Freddie and I did not see each other. I think it was the longest week of my life.

Then that August Sunday eventually arrived. It was like every other day of that glorious summer, the hottest of the century. The sun spilled a honeyed light over Golders Green synagogue as we

My wedding day, August 25, 1949. In the drab, uniform austerity of post-War Britain it had taken me many months of scouring the shops before I found the silver brocade for my bridal gown.

arrived. I was 20, and Freddie had celebrated his 27th birthday just
a month earlier. My cousin Sophie's two sons and two daughters
were my pages and bridesmaids. Freddie's cousin Ellen was the
third bridesmaid. His brother, Ernie, was the best man.

There were 400 guests thronging the synagogue, many from the
new State of Israel, others from America, France, Belgium, and
almost every other European country. The tables were invisible
below a field of white roses. Their sweet scent filled the building.

Freddie, strangely subdued and military-straight in his dinner
suit, saw me enter and his eyes creased in a smile. I fell in love with
him all over again.

After the ceremony there was an afternoon reception for all the
guests in the hall of the synagogue. And later that evening we held a
dinner for 250 of them in Folman's restaurant in the West End – the
only place for a Jewish society wedding party. The dinner, like
everything else in post-War Britain, was governed by restrictions.
For instance, only two courses were served. But we had wine and
traditional Jewish wedding music, with the joyous dances of our
culture.

And finally the new Mr. and Mrs. Freddie Breitfeld set off on
their honeymoon.

Tough currency rules were still in force, meaning that we were
allowed to take only £25 out of the country. That might seem a
ridiculously paltry sum these days, but it was amazing how far one
could go with £25 in those days.

We travelled first to Dover and then took the night boat train all
the way to the South of France. Our first stop was Juan les Pins on
the Riviera where we had a hotel looking out onto a near-empty
beach. It was a pretty little place, still clinging on to its identity as a

fishing village. Many years later *le jet set* would transform it into the bustling, over-priced resort it is today.

I remember it with tremendous fondness. Every night we dined on the finest fish dishes, because rationing was unknown there. We sat on our terrace, sipping pink champagne and listening to the waves lap against the beach. After all those months of preparation and flat-hunting we needed this tranquility.

We spent a week there before travelling just down the coast to San Remo and the aptly-named Royal Hotel. As honeymooners we were treated like royalty, and, amazingly, we still had most of our money left, so we indulged ourselves enormously.

Then disaster struck. At first it did not seem anything to worry about. It was just a single mosquito and it bit Freddie under the arm. When he was serving in the Far East with Mountbatten, he had been bitten thousands of times by mosquitoes, so he didn't make any song and dance about this particular bite.

But the next morning the angry little red mark had ballooned in size and Freddie was running a fever. I had no idea whether Riviera mosquitoes were malarial. All I knew was my bridegroom was stricken with some outlandish illness. The bite soon turned into a festering abscess.

I ignored his protestations and told the hotel to find me a doctor. They went one better than that. They found a professor. He came to the bridal suite carrying a huge black bag. He studied the abscess with grave eyes. I looked at Freddie and thought: "Oh dear, this must be serious."

Freddie looked at me and thought: "Can we afford to pay the man?"

The professor plunged in his bag and came up with a hypodermic needle. "Penicillin," he explained.

Penicillin! In 1949 penicillin was rarer than gold dust, and just about as expensive. Freddie groaned aloud, and his groan had nothing to do with the injection.

"Good," the professor announced. "This will cure it. And just to be certain, from now on a nurse will come in every day to give you another shot."

An even deeper groan from Freddie.

The professor hoisted up his bag and went away, leaving Freddie and me staring horror-stricken at each other. We knew there was absolutely no way our slender travel expenses could be stretched to pay for a course of penicillin, quite apart from the professor's fees *and* the cost of the daily nurse.

There was nothing else for it. I stopped eating. Gone were those lavish lunches and the sumptuous dinners. No more fine wines for us. Fortunately Freddie had lost his appetite, but I survived for days on a diet of bread rolls and mineral water. Even so, occasionally my nostrils would detect the mouth-watering aroma of *sole bonne femme* or *truite meuniere* emanating from the restaurant. I have always had a healthy appetite, and those moments were ones of sheer torture. But I gritted my teeth and thought of our precious little bundle of sterling.

Every morning the nurse, a brisk no-nonsense character, arrived to give Freddie his penicillin injection. She chattered away while we remained silent, wondering what her tender ministrations would cost us. Ten pounds? Twenty pounds? Certainly more than we could afford.

And then I thought about the casino, a very imposing, very fanciful building, which was what really put San Remo on the map. Before the mosquito had spoiled things, Freddie and I had gone there to see the seriously rich at play. We were not tempted to have a flutter ourselves, but we enjoyed the spectacle. Beneath the baroque ceiling and the gilded chandeliers, elegant women strung with more diamonds than Tiffany's and their handsome escorts casually tossed handfuls of 10,000-lira *jetons* onto the green baize. We watched fortunes – or fortunes to us anyway – being won or lost on a spin of the roulette wheel.

Now that Freddie was ill, my interest in the casino had nothing to do with the games of chance. I was concerned only with their money-changing rates. Did the casino, I wondered, offer the same astonishing black market exchange as the casino in Knokke had given me a few years earlier?

It did. I tendered my remaining English pounds, and in return I received the most enormous wad of lira. It was indeed an *embarasse de richesse*. Far too much even to cram into my handbag. I hurried back to the bridal suite and showed Freddie my spoils. He was thrilled. But it was still too early to celebrate.

The next morning the professor returned. He examined Freddie and pronounced him cured. Then he produced his bill. We took one look at it and almost had to stop ourselves from whooping out loud. I'm quite sure none of the professor's patients ever paid him so happily. My mosquito-bitten mate peeled off one note after another from our trove of lire. When he had settled the account in full, we still had a great pile of crisp notes. The doctor bade us farewell and went on his way.

"Now," said Freddie, still clutching a handful of lire. "What are we going to do with this?"

I knew exactly what. "Let's eat."

So we returned to our free-spending ways for the rest of the honeymoon and we stinted ourselves nothing. Even when the time came to leave San Remo, we had more money than we knew what to do with. Then one afternoon, browsing through the local shops, we chanced upon some very elegant wine glasses. We treated ourselves to our own wedding present – twelve glasses each for champagne, red wine, white wine and sherry. I still have the set almost intact.

We returned to London with an unspent sheaf of lire in Freddie's pocket.

As I said, it's amazing how far £25 went in those days.

A RECIPE FOR MARRIAGE

I embarked on married life determined to be an ideal wife. Our flat, I resolved, would become a home where all our friends and relatives would be welcome.

There was one major flaw in this grand plan. I couldn't boil an egg. Making toast was about the height of my culinary skills, and even then I wasn't terribly good at it. Nor had I the faintest idea of how to be a hostess. This called for serious consideration.

Freddie worked very hard and very late as he sought to build up his business. I also had a job, helping Papa sell trimmings to the textile trade. But at least I worked only normal office hours. So, when I came home in the evenings, I pored over recipes and recruited friends to teach me how to cook. It was a steep learning curve. Before long I was priding myself on my skills in the kitchen. And it was never a chore. I found right from the start that I really enjoyed cooking up something special from very little. Freddie played the role of guinea pig, sampling my latest recipes and pronouncing them successful or otherwise. And to be truthful, the poor man had to put up with quite a few culinary catastrophes before I got it right.

But I was nothing if not confident, and from the very start I initiated an open house every Sunday for friends and family. This began with a brunch and rolled on to high tea and later to evening cocktails. Throughout the day friends would come and go, but the chatter and laughter continued unabated. My girl friends were enormously impressed with Freddie's mother, Resi. Not only was she terribly chic and witty. She had also raised three gifted sons who combined brilliance with sensitivity. Everyone knew that the Breitfeld boys, who had come to Britain as refugees, were destined to become men of standing.

The three were also very close to each other. Later Ernest and Paul would join Freddie in the fur business. Each had his own particular talents to bring to the enterprise. Together they developed it into a textile business which eventually went public and was sold to one of the biggest companies in Britain.

They were frequent visitors to the flat, and if, as was often the case, they found themselves surrounded by admiring young women, they did not seem to find the ordeal too hard to bear.

We lived in Willesden Lane for seven years, years that I remember with unalloyed pleasure. If I had to summon up an image of those days, it would be of a Sunday, when the flat echoed to the voices of our friends. Over by the window Freddie and Papa are chuckling over something one of them has said. Then Freddie catches my eye and he smiles, just as he smiled that very first time in Claridge's. My world was utter and complete.

In the early years of our marriage I often accompanied Freddie on business trips. At that time his company was exclusively concerned with making rabbit fur gloves. They were an essential fashion accessory of the day, and just as important, rabbit fur was not subject to the hefty taxes which were imposed on other furs.

Every other weekend Freddie needed to go to Paris and talk to the agents who supplied him with rabbit pelts. The business side of things I left to him, and while he was off signing contracts and arranging shipments, I would go on window shopping expeditions around the boutiques of the Left Bank.

Our usual resting place was the Swiss Hotel on the Boulevard Haussman, which, we had learned through painful experience, was the only Parisian hotel in our price range that was not hopping with bed bugs. When Freddie's work for the day was done, we threw ourselves into enjoying the night life of Paris. These were heady times indeed, for Paris was still celebrating its liberation. Freddie and I would stroll through Montmartre, where music drifted from every other doorway and the pavement cafes echoed to the heated debates of poets, philosophers, artists and authors. It seemed as if the entire Left Bank was peopled by earnest young intellectuals, and each one had a totally diametric viewpoint from his neighbour.

Paris prided itself as the creative capital of the world, and with some justification. It boasted 130 major art galleries. New York had only 30. Some 60,000 artists – a third of them from America, Great Britain and other European nations – lived in the crowded web of narrow streets that straggled down to the banks of the Seine. Every year 2,000 artists staged exhibitions. There were almost as many different schools of thought as there were artists – the surrealists, led by Chagall, Braque's cubist disciples, and the fauvists who still rallied around Raoul Dufy. There were too the modernists, the post-modernists, the primitives, the *naifs* and the action painters. For artists, Paris was the only place to be.

It was much the same for writers. Before the War, Paris was home to James Joyce, Hemingway, Fitzgerald, Gertrude Stein, and a wealth of others. They had since died or fled from the Nazis. But now their tables in the cafes of the Place Pigalle were taken by equally illustrious figures.

The great Existentialist thinkers, Jean-Paul Sartre and Albert Camus, had spent their War years underground in the French Resistance. Now they were free again to practise their craft. Samuel Beckett, another hero of the Resistance, was evolving a new stark style of theatre. Between the can-can dance acts at the Folies Bergeres, Maurice Chevalier, with his trademark straw hat and cane, crooned love songs.

Not for us the high-stepping shows of the Folies. For Freddie was a jazz fiend. Swing, Dixieland, modern jazz, he loved it all. Our nightly excursions always ended up in one of the scores of cellar clubs where we drank *vin ordinaire* and danced to the legendary jazz bands. It was there I first heard Louis Armstrong and Count Basie. In the 'Twenties and 'Thirties Paris was the cradle of the Jazz Age, and now that it was liberated, all the great names of jazz made pilgrimages to the city. Amazingly, it cost little or nothing to enter these clubs, which was just as well, because in those days everyone seemed poor. But this was long before Paris turned into the expensive tourist trap it is today. The music, the poetry readings in the cafes, the paintings displayed on street corners were all part of the pageantry of this frantic beehive of artistic expression. We were of course unaware of it, but we were witnessing the birth of the Beatniks and their Beat Generation. We felt we were part of that vibrant atmosphere which established Paris as the heart of Bohemia. I quickly became used to the cabaret going on all around us.

But there was one particular sight that never ceased to astonish me. As in London, there was little in the way of fashion for young working class women. Yet sometimes in a smoky jazz club I would catch a glimpse of women dressed in skin-tight sweaters in the most dazzling colours imaginable. Where on earth did they get these fantastic creations?

A closer look revealed precisely why the "clothes" were so skin-tight: the women were absolutely naked. But to look fashionable, they had the garish "sweaters" painted on their bodies by their artist boyfriends. Modesty certainly took second place to *la mode*. It was a spectacle which always made me blink, but the Parisiennes took it in their stride.

We would stroll back to our hotel with Freddie humming a tune he had just picked up. I knew he was just itching to get home to London to play the tune on the organ in our lounge. It was a modest affair, but he derived enormous pleasure from it. After a hectic day

On the Lido at Venice. Freddie and I with Trudie Reiss and her husband Simon who had brought us together.

at the office, he loved to sit down at the organ and rattle through his repertoire, with his sleeves rolled up and a blissful smile on his face.

Gradually he began to gather other instruments, such as a harmonica and a guitar. And soon the Willesden Lane flat became the venue for jam sessions as friends turned up to join in the music-making. I loved music too, but I was content to listen. To be frank, I don't think my contribution would have been appreciated, for I was tone deaf.

Freddie had a wide coterie of friends, some of them quite remarkable people. One in particular. He was another Freddie. Freddie Knoller. Not only did they share the same first name, they once shared a double desk at school in Vienna and they were the best of friends. But during the War they lost contact.

Then one night the phone rang with a long distance call from Baltimore. Freddie Knoller was on the line, filling in all the gaps since last they had seen each other. He was a survivor of the camps. He had been caught in a police round-up in France and imprisoned in a holding centre. From there he was transported to Germany and a harrowing spell as a slave labourer in the I.G. Farben armaments plant. When he had outlived his usefulness there, he was sent on to Belsen to die. But Freddie was saved in the nick of time when British troops liberated the camp.

After the War he married Frieda, an Englishwoman, and the couple moved to the States. There they might have stayed but for Frieda's father who offered to set him up in a business in England. So they came to London and the two Freddies were reunited.

Freddie Knoller was every bit as interesting, as amusing, as intelligent as my Freddie had always pictured him. And Frieda was a wonderfully warm and easy person. Overnight I suddenly had two very special friends. And thus they have remained.

The Knollers set up in the retail business, did extremely well for themselves and later sold out. But not for Freddie a life of quiet retirement. He became the British director of Israel Bonds, and he is also very active in running the Holocaust Survivors' Centre in Hendon. Freddie's own story of survival in Belsen is so dramatic that the great movie director Stephen Spielberg used it in his documentary on the Holocaust.

After a couple of years, I had to give up our weekends in Paris for the very good reason that I was pregnant. Our son, Michael was born on the 13th of January, 1952 at the Welbeck Street Clinic. We gave his Jewish name as Moishe, after my maternal grandfather. Michael's arrival might have been better timed, for it coincided with the last great smog of London. Sometimes I watch an old movie, depicting the streets of London swirling with fog. Anyone who has not experienced the real thing might think the misty scene romantic and mysterious. But for those who had to put up with these peasoupers, they were at best dreadful, at worst, deadly.

What happened was that a cold current of air trapped all the smoke and fumes pouring from millions of chimneys and pushed it back down into the streets. One could not see more than a few yards, even at noon. This lack of visibility and the stinging eyes were but minor inconveniences compared to the smog's other effects. The air was laden with microscopic particles of toxic sulphur and nitrous oxide. They triggered epidemics of bronchitis, asthma and pneumonia. Hundreds, even thousands of Londoners died in each poison cloud.

This one lingered for two weeks. I was back home again but I was slowly choking to death from the fumes, so I was sent to Bournemouth where I could breathe freely. The move almost broke my heart, for it meant I was parted from my baby. I stayed in Bournemouth only a week and every night I cried myself to sleep.

Michael, meanwhile, was in our flat and under the solicitous care of his nurse, Edith. She was an Austrian woman with a great deal of commonsense and experience. She was also devoted to Michael.

While I was pining for my baby in Bournemouth, the Government was finally doing something about these awful smogs which blighted London every winter. They passed the Clean Air Act, which decreed that only smokeless fuel could be used in cities. With that one stroke smog was forever banished from the streets and London could breathe easily again.

I returned to Willesden Lane to find that Michael was not feeding properly. He was failing to gain weight and there was real concern for his health. The paediatrician made various recommendations but nothing seemed to work. And then Edith hit on the solution. She remembered a recipe for soured milk which had been in use in Austria. Edith made it up in the kitchen, filled a bottle for Michael, and to our heartfelt relief, he took to it from the very first sip.

Before long he was gaining a pound a week and the danger was over. My paediatrician was so impressed he asked Edith for the recipe and then he approached Cow and Gate, the largest baby food company in Britain. They were equally impressed. Using Edith's formula, they produced Lacidac, a powdered substitute, and they kept Michael supplied with it for as long as he needed it. Soon it was on sale in chemist shops all over Britain. It's still on sale today, helping a new generation of reluctant eaters to develop into healthy babies. And they owe it all to Edith. I know that I am forever in her debt because, without her help, God knows how Michael might have fared.

A small postscript here: Michael is no longer the food faddist he was when he was a little boy. I learned this to my cost after a family reunion at a Bar Mitzvah in Jerusalem in 1970. Relatives from Venezuela, America, Europe and all over the globe had flocked to the occasion. It was the ceremony for my cousin Ben's oldest son, Alex. Ben's mother was my Aunt Ella who had hidden Siche all those years ago in Berlin.

For many of the guests this was the first time they had been to Israel and I thought we should all have a day's sightseeing together. So on the Sunday of the Bar Mitzvah weekend, I hired a coach. Just before the party set off, Michael suggested that he invite some of his friends from Jerusalem university for lunch while we were on our day's outing. The understanding was of course that I was to pick up the bill. We readily agreed, thinking it would be nice if Michael treated three or four of his student pals to lunch.

That evening a weary – and ravenously hungry – coachload of day trippers returned to the hotel, only to be greeted by the manager with the words: "Sorry. We have nothing to eat."

I said: "What do you mean – nothing?"

He said: "Nothing. That's what I mean. Your son and his friends have eaten me out of house and home."

I was bemused. How could a small group of students eat everything in the hotel? I asked.

Now it was the manager's turn to be shocked. "Small group! Your son had 26 guests for lunch."

But back to his fraught early days. I returned to work, leaving the baby in Edith's tender care. She always dressed in the smart blue uniform of a nurse. When it was time for Michael's daily walk, she would don her cape, put him in the navy blue pram, and wheel him around the park. One very rarely saw a proper nurse with a baby in those days. There was something almost regal about the way she promenaded with him. It reminded one of the newspaper photographs of a nurse wheeling the infant Prince Charles in St. James Park. And that prompted Freddie to dub his son Prince Michael of Breitfeld.

The title did not last long because Freddie chose to Anglicize his family name to Bradfield. His brother, Ernie, was in the Merchant Navy and away on the high seas at the time so he couldn't be told. Only later, when he returned, did we discover that Ernie too had changed his name, in his case to Debrett. Paul had also opted for Debrett. Later still, the two younger brothers trimmed their names down to Brett, thus, when the three boys eventually formed a partnership, it was known as Bradfield, Brett & Co.

Michael, after his traumatic first few months, was turning into a healthy and handsome baby. He had inherited his father's calm nature.

On the 5th of August, 1955, I was back in the Welbeck Street Clinic for the birth of our first daughter, Vita. The name came from her grandmother and it also signified Life. It seemed to suit her, because she was so full of life. Freddie and I were overjoyed. We had no idea of the heartache to come.

By now the flat which we once thought so spacious was becoming a trifle cramped for our growing family. We decided to buy our first house. It cost us £5,400 – a sizeable sum in the mid-fifties, but we were certain it was worth it. Then we hit a snag.

The landlord refused to let us sell off the lease to our flat. We were in a real predicament because we could not afford to keep two homes going. Eventually we came up with an audacious plan. If the landlord would not let us sell, we would buy the entire block of flats from him and we could then do whatever we wanted. For the plan to succeed, we needed financial help from other members of our families. They were unstinting in their support and we were able to buy the block and sell it on so that we could buy the house.

I always feel a warm glow when I think about our first house. It was large, detached, and it had four bedrooms – one of a group of nine identical houses which had just been built at Hendon. By happy chance all our neighbours were of the same age and of the same backgrounds as ours. They too had children, and although we had never met our neighbours before, they were soon firm friends. There was a true sense of community among us. And of course the children instantly formed friendships. Vita, with her long, light brown curls and clear blue eyes, was a golden child. She was not even three years old but she had already found a boyfriend in the child next door. Michael had begun classes at the local Jewish school and was proving a keen student. But he was terribly thin for his age, largely because he was scarcely eating. No matter what I prepared for him, he would take only a few forkfuls and that was sufficient. He was much too old now for Edith's miraculous cure and his lack of appetite worried me greatly. Then one day I gave him a sliver of smoked salmon. To my astonishment, he asked for more. And more. We'd found the answer, a rather expensive answer, but I didn't care. It is true to say that we raised Michael on a diet of smoked salmon.

Vita too gave us cause for concern. She had adenoid problems which caused her breathing difficulties. We took her to the top specialist in the field who pronounced that a minor operation would cure the adenoid trouble. Freddie and I decided she should have the operation and we booked her into the Royal Ear, Nose and Throat Hospital in Gray's Inn Road. I drove Vita down to hospital, repeating what the doctors had said. It was just a minor operation. She was wearing her little white rabbit coat, the coat she was so proud of. She was just two years and ten months old. Freddie and I were not taking any chances and we had retained the services of a surgeon with a glowing reputation. All along, everyone stressed this was just routine surgery. It was performed dozens of times every day in hospitals all over the country.

But this time something went wrong.

In those days mothers were not allowed to stay in hospital with their children. I phoned when Vita was still on the operating table. By then she was already gone. In the midst of this minor operation, an embolism had formed, causing her heart to fail.

I rang Freddie and got a neighbour to drive me to the hospital. Everyone – our friends and relatives – arrived soon afterwards. I was utterly beside myself with grief. How could my daughter, so golden, so quick with life, be dead? It was too terrible a tragedy to believe.

Afterwards there were the traditional seven days and seven nights of *Shiva* at our home. All of our friends and acquaintances came to pay their respects. There were so many people that the queue stretched from our front door right into the next street. Everyone was in a state of shock that such a little child had been plucked from life.

We were shown tremendous kindness and love by all we knew. But Freddie and I were inconsolable. We had lost Vita and nothing in the world would ever make up for that, nor could time ease the pain.

In my heart, the grief and the sense of loss are still as sharp today.

Our beloved Vita who brought us such joy, and whose loss was a lasting tragedy.

WOMEN OF PROPERTY

In the late 'fifties the Czech Government in Exile paid us two thirds of the money which Papa had lodged in the Central Bank in Prague before the War. Paula and I suddenly found ourselves the possessors of quite a large amount of money. The question was: how were we going to use it? We discussed various enterprises, but the one area which caught our imagination was property. Admittedly, but for that one brief foray into real estate when Freddie and I bought the Willesden Lane block, we had no experience. That did not set us back, for Paula and I both had bags of confidence. Plus there was still a shortage of rented accommodation in London. We were bound to succeed. That is how we felt anyway, and both Freddie and Paula's husband, Zeev, went along with it.

Our first venture had a decidedly mixed outcome. We found a man who was very keen to sell his house on Hampstead Heath. We agreed a price and signed all the papers. We had our very first property.

But not for long. The seller, to his dismay, realised he could not find any other house he wanted to buy. He offered to buy the house back from us. Paula and I thought hard about it. We knew if we held on to it we had a very sound investment on our hands. But we also felt sorry for the poor seller who was by now homeless. And so we sold it back at a small profit. That was the first £500 we had ever made. If we'd been ruthless businesswomen we would have made a great deal more, but we felt happier doing it this way.

In the meantime Freddie and his brothers had diversified. Instead of making gloves, they were now in the curtain business. In those days everybody, from the highest to the lowest, wanted net curtains for their windows. They bought a length of net material and had someone sew it up for them. But Bradfield, Brett & Co. had a better idea – to sell the curtains already made up. They marketed their wares through mail order, pioneers in this new way of selling.

Freddie, the one-time penniless refugee, rapidly overcame his faltering start in Britain to become a captain of industry.

The idea was an instant success and the company, launched by three boys who arrived in Britain as almost destitute refugees, soon found itself in the big league. The profits were immense and many years later, in the 'Seventies, the firm was bought up by Reed International, who owned the fabrics giant Sandersons.

❖ ❖ ❖

Almost a year after Vita died, I gave birth to a second daughter, Cherry, on the 23rd of March, 1959. For obvious reasons we fussed and fretted over her, and her grandparents indulged her enormously. There was never any danger that Cherry would grow into a spoiled child, because right from the start she had a strong independent streak, which Freddie blamed on me.

Cherry grew quickly into a tall and beautiful girl. She was a very fast learner and a born organiser. And she was always at the centre of whatever was going on. I recall her sitting in her pink-decorated bedroom and holding court for all her many friends.

Michael too was constantly surrounded by playmates, and sometimes the house seemed crammed to the rafters with children. The friends that Michael and Cherry made in Hendon are still close to them today.

With business booming, Freddie began planning his dream house, a dream he had long cherished. The first move was in 1962 when he bought a large plot in Bishop's Avenue, Hampstead, the most exclusive address in north London. The site alone cost us £30,000, an absolute fortune in those days.

Once he had found the place to build the dream house, Freddie set about planning its every feature. As I've said, he was always a frustrated architect and now he had the opportunity to show off his

Michael's ninth birthday party.
He had already planned his career – to work alongside his father.

creative flair. He enlisted Ivan King, the foremost film and TV set designer of the time, to help make the dream a reality. Among King's many credits were that he was the set designer on the top TV series, *The Saint*, starring a very youthful Roger Moore.

The planning alone took Freddie and Ivan King two years before a single brick was laid. There were so many decisions to make. I wanted lots and lots of bedrooms so that we could have guests. Freddie wanted an enormous lounge for his now-regular jam sessions. Naturally, we needed the most modern of kitchens. And of course a dining room capable of seating 20 people. Our dreams spiralled...

In 1966, four years after we bought the site, the house was completed at a cost of £70,000. Our ideal home was now ready for us, but we were not quite ready for it. We had the rather important matter of Michael's Bar Mitzvah to attend to first. Michael had spent all his young life in Hendon. His friends were there, as indeed were our friends. We felt very much a part of the local community and it seemed disloyal to uproot ourselves at such an important time. So our new house lay vacant for six months and we did not move in until after the Bar Mitzvah ceremony at Hendon United Synagogue.

The house in Bishops Avenue was a tall, imposing building with a wide frontage looking out onto the leafy avenue. Its three storeys contained 6,500 square feet of space. There were five bedrooms on the first floor and another two and a huge playroom on the top floor.

The house was built in rustic brick and stone. The style was modern, but understated. The grand front door opened onto a generous hall which led in turn to a vast split level lounge. In one corner of this was Freddie's baby grand piano, and beside it was a great trunk containing saxophones, clarinets, harmonicas, trumpets, and all sorts of instruments for visitors to play during the jam sessions.

I think the *coup de grace* was the magnificent staircase which curved up in a wide majestic sweep to the first floor gallery. Simply walking down that staircase, dressed for an evening out, made one feel like a princess. The staircase also played a major part in the charity fashion shows I had begun to organise. The guests would sit in the lounge and watch the models parade the latest fashions down our staircase. When each new mannequin appeared at the top of the flight, there was always a sudden chorus of Oohhs! and Aahhs! It was that dramatic.

At the rear of the lounge, framed by dark orange silk curtains, French windows opened on to landscaped gardens which were every bit in keeping with the house. In summer the scene resembled a hotel garden, with dozens of guests in gaily-striped deckchairs chatting away the afternoon.

Cherry's organisational instinct came to the fore when we threw a grand Guy Fawkes Night party in the garden, inviting scores of friends. She said: "Why don't we charge everyone admission?"

Freddie blinked.

Cherry explained: "If we charged everyone a shilling (five pence in today's money), we could give the money to charity."

And that's precisely what we did. Though our guests generously chipped in rather more than the shilling-a-head which Cherry had envisaged.

I was still engaged in running the property business with Paula. We had dozens of tenants in properties all over North London and we prided ourselves on running a sound and respectable service. But in the early 'Sixties, a scandal broke which was to spoil everything. The newspapers exposed a thoroughly unscrupulous,

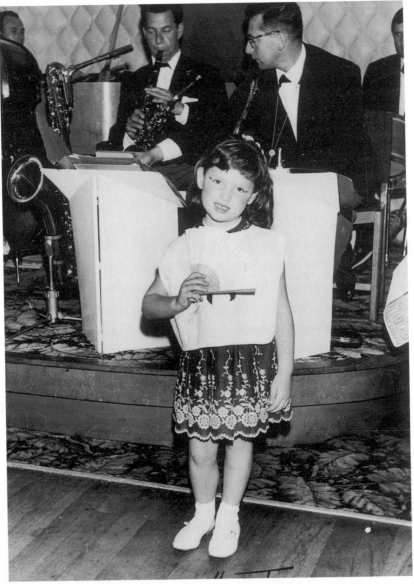

Mademoiselle Butterfly – Cherry was never happier than when she was dressing up and acting, a trait shared by her own daughter, Miriel.

and indeed violent, landlord called Peter Rachman. His practice was to impose massive rent increases on tenants, and, when they were unable to pay, he sent his hired thugs to terrorise them. Helpless tenants were brutally beaten up and warned that if they complained to the police, they would be killed.

When the story broke it exposed a gaping hole in Britain's rent laws, whereby the landlord could charge whatever he wanted and the tenant did not have any rights. Details of Rachman's nasty little empire filled the newspapers for months, and gave the English language a new word, Rachmanism, meaning brutal extortion. Questions were raised in Parliament and the upshot of it all was that overnight the terms landlord and landlady became dirty words. Our letting business had always been responsible, but with Freddie's company about to go public, I felt it wiser to bow out of the rental business. I sold my half of the company to Paula.

Within months, the Government had pushed through the Rent Act, giving tenants the protection they deserved.

The public flotation of Bradfield, Brett & Co. on the stock exchange was an undreamed-of success. When news of the planned flotation went around, everybody was anxious to congratulate the three brothers. There was a communal sense of pride that three refugee boys had through their own hard work and acumen forged a public company. It was unheard of, hence all the excitement.

So many people were asking, no, demanding to see the brothers that I resolved to throw two enormous parties. In the morning I invited all the friends of our own generation and literally hundreds flocked to the house in Hendon. Freddie, Ernie and Paul found themselves lionised as one by one the guests came forward to shake their hands. Everyone was convinced the public flotation would be a tremendous triumph. After all, the brothers had already demonstrated how they could fashion a great enterprise out of nothing.

In the afternoon, as soon as the guests had departed, I got the house back in order and then it was time to open the doors again and welcome a second huge party. This time the guests were from our parents' generation. They were just as numerous as those we had entertained in the morning and equally as effusive.

Naturally everyone wanted to buy shares in the new venture. I'm afraid many were disappointed, because the stock was twenty times oversubscribed. That in itself displays just how confident people were in the brothers' skills. The investors' faith in them was richly rewarded as the shares soared in value.

Now that I was no longer wrapped up in the day-to-day running of the property business, I found myself with time on my hands. But not for long. I remembered those *Shabbos* evenings of my childhood in Berlin, when Papa would sit at the walnut dining table, recounting stories from the *shtetl*. One lesson that he had always impressed upon us was the role of the rich man in the *shtetl*. His wealth conferred upon him the responsibility of looking after those less fortunate. Freddie and I were now more than comfortably well off and we had always been involved with charities in one way or another. After all, it was through my work with the Three C's charity that I had met Freddie.

But I felt the time had come to devote my energies to doing more. Quite coincidentally someone else was thinking the same. Her name was Judy Goldkorn and she was a pivotal figure on the fund-raising side of WIZO, the Women's International Zionist

Organisation. She was, if you like, a talent spotter, ever on the look out for new recruits.

Our paths crossed at a WIZO bazaar in the Empire Rooms on Tottenham Court Road – where Paula and I had celebrated VE Day years earlier. I was in charge of a stall, selling shirts, and I was doing a roaring trade. (I like to think that I had inherited some of Papa's entrepreneurial skills.) Anyway, Judy was impressed. She came across, introduced herself and asked if I would like to join WIZO. She said I could work with babies and children and women in need of help.

The offer came at a most appropriate time. I was still trying to come to terms with the loss of Vita the year before, and I was very receptive to the idea that I might be able to help other children. I felt that here was something meaningful I could do, and that was a very pleasing thought. I said "Yes" to Judy immediately, and so began more than four decades of work with WIZO. I say work, but that doesn't do it justice, especially later. Every day was different. Sometimes it was frantic, often frustrating, invariably demanding, frequently exciting, and always, *always* hugely rewarding. I relished every moment of it.

I started off in a small way, as chairwoman of Chanita, the local chapter in Hendon. Under the guise of various social functions, ranging from Tupperware parties to bridge evenings, jumble sales to quiz nights, we raised much-needed funds for WIZO. I had become deeply interested in the organisation itself. It was founded by a wonderfully charismatic woman, Rebecca Sieff, whose son, Marcus, was later to become the head of Marks & Spencer. Her vision and tireless campaigning had turned it into a global organisation, so that by the time I joined there were fifty federations around the world and a total membership of more than 250,000 women. WIZO was really the mother of the infant State of Israel. Nowadays, when people talk of "girl power" as if it were a recent development, I allow myself a wry smile and think of Rebecca Sieff.

My interest and my modest successes in Hendon did not go unnoticed by Judy Goldkorn. She was my guru, always there with advice and encouragement. Now she felt I was ready to assume a greater role and she talked me into joining the fund raising department at WIZO's head office in Gloucester Place. I did not need much persuasion.

At head office I found myself surrounded by a group of brilliant and dedicated women. The most outstanding figure of all was the WIZO president, Elaine Blond, Rebecca Sieff's youngest sister. I was quite frankly in awe of Elaine, for here was the woman whose crusading zeal drove the *Kindertransport*. Close on ten thousand children owed their lives to her. And I was one of them.

Elaine had a reputation for being very prickly, very autocratic. This was not quite fair. She had a wholesome disrespect for officialdom and petty bureaucracy, a disrespect born no doubt from those grim pre-War days when almost single-handedly she had taken on the massed ranks of Whitehall's pen pushers. Elaine had learned quickly that soft words and earnest pleas cut no ice whatsoever with the civil service mentality. So she had resorted to hectoring, badgering, harrassing and generally bullying the bureaucrats until she got her way. And no one can question that the ends certainly justified the means.

Now Israel was a free and independent state, and her legendary battles with British officialdom were long in the past, but Elaine retained an air of *hauteur*. There was something of *la Grande Dame* in her demeanour, and her imperiousness on occasions intimidated many of those around her.

But as I came to know her, I realised that what was often mistaken for arrogance was simply her refusal to suffer fools gladly. Underneath that forbidding exterior, Elaine was a woman of tremendous kindness and loyalty. Once she recognised that you shared her passion and commitment to the cause of WIZO, you were a friend for life. I am proud to say she took me under her wing and we became very dear friends. Freddie and I were often invited to Gotwick Manor, her magnificent Tudor-style house, in East Grinstead. I think the fact that I was one of her *Kindertransport* protegees meant that she looked upon me almost as a daughter. It goes without saying that she was wonderful at her job. Elaine's death in 1985 left a hole in WIZO, a hole that has never been filled.

She encouraged me in my efforts in the fund-raising department, but she did not tell me how to do my job. She trusted me to deliver the goods. From the outset, I had formed my own philosophy. It was basically this: I would never ask anyone for money unless I felt they could afford to give. It worked and the donations kept rolling in. If ever I found out that a junior colleague had pressed someone into giving more than he or she could, I immediately paid it back. It was very important that we did not alienate our community.

After a few years on the team, I was invited to become co-chairwoman of the FRC, the fund-raising committee. It was a role I was privileged to fill for almost twenty years.

Among the early challenges we faced was coping with the aftermath of Operation Magic Carpet, when 40,000 Yemenite Jews were suddenly spirited to Israel. It was a tremendous tactical coup, but it posed untold welfare problems.

For much of that time in the FRC, the other co-chairwoman was Doris Lewis who was somewhat older than I but ve hit it off instantly. Our friendship and WIZO went hand in hand and over the years we worked in perfect harmony together, raising many millions of pounds. The money was sorely needed, for most immigrants to Israel arrived with little more than a cardboard suitcase and a few old clothes. Some lacked even that. Therefore the demands on WIZO were unceasing. And apart from the day-to-day problems of clothing and feeding the new citizens, there were frequent emergencies. At Yom Kippur in October 1973, specially-trained Egyptian forces crossed the Suez Canal and attacked the Bar Lev defensive line, invading deep into Sinai. Simultaneously in the north, the Syrians attacked on the Golan Heights. The twin strikes came without warning, and the raiders made rapid advances before Israel mounted a daring counter attack, leapfrogging the Egyptian paratroop forces in Sinai and attacking them from the rear. Within a few weeks, the Israeli soldiers had crushed the enemy's much vaunted tank regiments and were on the brink of an even greater victory when Egypt wisely negotiated a ceasefire. The peril on Israel's borders was vanquished, for the time being anyway, but victory had come at a heavy cost in human lives and also in damaged aircraft, armour and military installations. The outcome of this was that the national budget was given over to rebuilding the defences. And that in turn meant there was no money for the new immigrants, or indeed for general welfare work. This was where WIZO once again came to the rescue.

We staged galas, fashion shows, charity concerts, auctions. There were bequests and trust funds. I had the idea for a giant Jumborama to be held at Alexandra Palace. I rang around all my many contacts, coaxing them into donating second hand clothes, unwanted furniture, books, musical instruments, even *objets d'art*, and they responded magnificently. I designed logos and notepaper, worked out advertising, and sent thousands of invitations. Then two weeks before the date set for the biggest jumble sale that Britain had ever seen, the Alexandra Palace was badly damaged by fire. But we ploughed on regardless, staging the great Jumborama in a part of the building which had escaped the blaze. I cannot recall exactly how much we raised, but it was way above our highest expectations.

My speciality in the fund raising team was always the organisational side. I had a long list of people – tycoons, stars, musicians – I knew I could always cajole into helping the cause. Each time I launched an appeal, I did it for a specific purpose, and it was always something emotive. I believed that helped encourage would-be donors. They knew that their pounds and pence were going directly to relieve a specific problem. The only trouble was that Israel had so many such problems. But I loved the bustle of the office, and above all, I loved the thought that we were doing something truly worthwhile. I devoted more and more time to the Fund Raising Committee, and Freddie, who recognised how much it meant to me, was constantly supportive.

The FRC was often called on to perform miracles, as in 1985, in the wake of Operation Moses, when 12,000 Ethiopian Jews were airlifted to Israel. Their plight was even greater than that of the earlier immigrants from Yemen. For the most part, these newcomers were almost naked. They lacked food, money, education, health care. Many of the children were desperately ill with rheumatic fever. Again it fell to WIZO to tend the refugees. And so we embarked on another hectic round of fund raising. Among our first priorities was the setting up of a clinic in Jerusalem to treat the sick children. Then we needed to establish a network of creches, where healthy children could be cared for while their

Meeting the then President of Israel, Ephraim Katzir, during a British WIZO visit to Tel Aviv.

mothers were learning the rudiments of hygiene, cooking, welfare and even women's rights. It was important to integrate them as soon as possible into the modern State of Israel.

In Britain, Doris Lewis and I recruited stars like Frankie Vaughan, Helen Shapiro and that wonderfully generous man, David Jacobs, to help spearhead our various campaigns. Just as we thought we were getting to grips with things, a new emergency sprung up. Among the Ethiopian Jews were several hundred young people who were presently housed in a sea-front hotel at Netanya. They had been earmarked for university, but the girls had only makeshift dresses and the boys were clad in ragged shorts. They did not even have underwear. Obviously there was no way this rag-tag army of youngsters could go to university unless they were properly clothed. The problem was made worse in that they were due to enroll in college a few weeks later.

But where on earth could I find sufficient underwear in time? In desperation I rang Maurice Cresswell, a friend in Nottingham who was in the textile business and I explained my predicament.

He asked: "Underwear for how many?"

"Thousands," I said.

There was a sharp intake of breath. Then Maurice said: "Leave it to me."

He got in touch with all his clothing contacts and within a fortnight, hundreds of boxes containing mostly undergarments and nightwear were delivered to the Gloucester Place head office. We hurriedly repacked them in ten giant trunks. El Al promised to transport them without charge and, with the trunks in the hold, a few of my WIZO colleagues and I flew off to deliver the goods. I must say I felt pretty pleased with myself.

The delight on the young people's faces when they saw their clothes is something that made all our efforts worthwhile.

In Netanya I met a remarkable man, a pensioner who had gone to Israel to spend his retirement there. He had worked hard all his days and he deserved a rest. But he had come out of retirement to act as a tireless worker on behalf of the young newcomers. He told me: "They came here naked. It is February now and the weather is too cold for them. I must do something."

So he had dedicated his days to being the clothing outfitter for the children in the several absorption centres around Netanya. He had contacted manufacturers of everything from tee shirts to suits, begging their help. And they had given it. In one of the hotels he had a vast area set aside as a clothes warehouse. But there was one critical gap in his stocks – he just could not get enough shoes, and he refused to let the children run around in ill-fitting shoes. "It will harm their feet," he said.

His answer was to launch a Shoe Fund. I was deeply impressed and I rushed back to the other delegates at a British WIZO conference in Netanya. I said: "Right, I want a fiver from each of you for this shoe fund."

They gave a great deal more than that. When we returned to London I told my son, Michael, about the man and his scheme. He was equally impressed, and he went round his many friends soliciting contributions. I was also proud of the part Michael played as a volunteer helper in the Yom Kippur War. He and four of his friends flew to Israel and used our family Volvo estate as an ambulance, driving up and down the Golan Heights and ferrying the walking wounded to hospital. He used to phone us at five in the morning and give us a running commentary as the huge Hercules transport planes flew in, laden with relief supplies.

Michael was enjoying his work so much that I had no little difficulty in prising him loose in time for the wedding of his cousin Zena, Paula's daughter, a few weeks later.

The work that WIZO carried out in response to Operation Moses paid handsome dividends. Many of the young people we had helped went on, as planned, to university and emerged as qualified teachers, engineers, scientists, doctors. They now play their full part as citizens of Israel, and they in turn help other newcomers.

There were many other demands for our help, as when there was a mass exodus of Moroccan Jews to Israel, or again when we began seeing the first influx from the old Soviet Union. Every emigrant had different needs and the calls for help were always urgent.

On occasion I found myself playing a role more as a diplomat than a fund raiser. In the early eighties I was petitioning for new child centres in Israel. Our concern was for children who needed the help of psychologists, and Elaine Blond had devised plans for pilot schemes. WIZO could supply the child psychologists and staff for the centres. Now all we needed was the funding.

Through a senior official in UNICEF, I was given an introduction to one of the world's largest charitable trusts, Van Leer in the Netherlands. I flew to Holland and went to their headquarters in the Hague. We had a convivial lunch and the Van Leer people listened politely as I outlined our requirements. They were not particularly keen to help. As they explained it, Van Leer's work largely consisted of feeding the starving of the Third World. They supplied bowls of rice to millions. I listened just as politely as they talked of Bangladesh, Ethiopia, the Sudan, India, and the terrible poverty of the underdeveloped nations. Then I said: "Poverty has many faces." And I spoke of the need to help the children in Israel.

Something must have got through because they gave their approval to supporting the centre – but only provided we had the full backing of the Histadrut in Israel. The Histadrut is a workers' cooperative, which has no real equivalent anywhere else in the world. The closest approximation I can think of is the old Soviet commune. The Histadrut is also very firmly leftist, and it identifies exclusively with the working class. The Van Leer people in Israel worked closely with the organisation, and I was warned that unless the Histadrut gave its blessing we would not receive any funding. I thanked the Van Leer people and returned to Britain. I did not foresee any problems. Surely a brief chat with Histadrut officials would secure clearance.

The next stage was to fly to Israel and see them. The first inkling of trouble ahead came as I was leaving our London apartment. Michael joined me in the lift and said: "Mum, I want you to know one thing about the Histadrut: they are not like other people. Believe me, I have met them. Don't take anything for granted. They will be very difficult."

I was still convinced it would be plain sailing. After all, the underprivileged and underachieving children our pilot programmes were designed to help lived in impoverished areas. Surely the Histadrut would welcome such support, especially as they did not have to pay a penny towards it. All they had to do was agree we could use a few municipal sites for the centres.

The venue for the meeting was the Hilton Hotel in Tel Aviv. Our small WIZO delegation included the international fund raising chairwoman and the head of its children's division. We ordered up tea and sandwiches and waited for the Histadrut representatives. Presently two men arrived. They each appeared to be five feet square, barrel-chested and tough. Our chairwoman asked them if they would prefer tea or coffee.

"Gin," one of them barked.

The chairwoman turned to the waiter. "Two *large* gins, please."

"A *bottle* of gin," the senior Histadrut man corrected her.

They got their bottle of gin and as they drank their way through it the chairwoman outlined the plans. Every suggestion she made was met with a curt "No!" These men didn't just look like brick walls, they acted like them.

At length they finished the gin and we had got precisely nowhere. I felt bitterly frustrated. Our cherished plans had just been stymied by a couple of gin-guzzling No-men.

But the chairwoman, who had a finely tuned sense of mischief, was undismayed. She said evenly: "You've just drunk a bottle of gin, telling us what we can't do. If I order you another bottle, will you tell us what we *can* do?"

It was so cheeky I almost laughed out loud. But the Histadrut men took it seriously. Another bottle of gin appeared on the table and it seemed to oil the wheels. Yes, the men agreed, the centres were a good idea. By the time the second bottle was finished, we had a deal. We could run two pilot schemes with their backing. So, with a little ingenuity and a lot of gin, we got them launched.

In London, my work in head office continued apace and the functions we organised became more and more glittering. There were operas at the Royal Covent Garden Opera House, headlined by stars like Placido Domingo and Jose Carreras. There were many concerts at the Royal Festival Hall, including some by the Israel Philharmonic Orchestra under Zubin Metha. WIZO recitals at the Royal Albert Hall featured a galaxy of internationally-renowned artists, among them Zuckerman, Barenboim, Grapelli, Oistrakh. That gracious hotel, the Cumberland, played host to bazaars. There were black-tie evenings, gala balls, a never-ending programme of events.

But two moments in particular stand out, both of them luncheons at the Guildhall. The first, in 1980 was to commemorate the diamond aniversary of the founding of WIZO. Because it was such a special day, we had the City's priceless hoard of gold on display, and this along with the regalia and the uniforms, ensured the occasion was dressed in pomp and circumstance. The guests were equally elevated. Our luncheon was attended by the Sheriff and aldermen and all the leading figures in the City. Its guest of honour was Chaim Herzog, the immediate former Israeli ambassador to the United Nations, and the man who was soon to become President of Israel. I recall looking around that magnificent banquetting hall, filled with such important personages and reflecting how far WIZO had come in the sixty years since Rebecca Sieff had founded it. She launched the organisation in the teeth of fierce opposition from male-dominated Zionist groups. Now here were all these great men happy to pay tribute to Rebecca's vision.

The co-chairwoman of the fund raising committee was Lily, Lady Sieff, who was also a close friend. A very glamorous and highly intelligent woman, she was the undoubted leading lady of Britain's Jewish community. Her husband, Lord Sieff, was the chairman of Marks & Spencer, which had been founded by his father, the first Lord Sieff. His mother was none other than Rebecca Sieff. Lily was a great patron of the arts and a renowned society hostess. Cabinet Ministers, internationally acclaimed artists and leading industrialists all enjoyed her lavish hospitality at dinner parties where Lady Sieff always sparkled. Her looks, her impeccable good taste, gave the impression that Lily, Lady Sieff was to the manor born. Yet she had the most astonishing story to tell of her early humble upbringing in Poland.

When the Nazi *Blitzkrieg* was unleashed upon the country, her parents gathered up their children and fled. The entire family slipped through the German lines in 1940 and across the border into Czechoslovakia. Hiding by day, and travelling by night, they walked south, living off berries and whatever scraps of food they could find. Theirs was truly an incredible journey for all of eastern Europe was an armed camp and no-one could be trusted. After several months of this precarious existence, ten-year-old Lily and her family finally reached Romania, and from there they sailed to Palestine. By the time they reached their safe haven, they were all barely more than skeletons.

The story of Lily's rise from penniless refugee to become the First Lady of Jewish society was one which inspired in me a tremendous admiration.

I recall at the Guildhall function how she was called upon to propose the loyal toast, after which I rose to propose the toast to Israel. She was at one end of the head table, and I at the other. After we had completed the toasts, quite spontaneously we turned to face each other and we simultaneously raised our glasses in a silent tribute. I was remembering the little girl who had dodged the Nazis across Europe, and she was remembering how I too had fled as a refugee.

The second Guildhall celebration several years later was a luncheon to honour the then Prime Minister, Margaret Thatcher. In the run-up to the function, we succeeded in raising one and a quarter million pounds which was subsequently used to build the Margaret Thatcher WIZO Women's Centre at Sderot, in the south of Israel. Another triumph for women's power!

I have personal memories too which are forever with me, as when WIZO made me an honorary vice-president. And again when I was presented with the Rebecca Sieff Award, the highest honour which WIZO can bestow. The citation read: "For devoted and outstanding service rendered to the cause of WIZO in the spirit of its founder."

I gave up my role on the fund-raising committee in the late 'Eighties because I felt it was time I moved over and let a younger generation contribute its energies, its ideas. But WIZO and its activities are still very dear to my heart.

HOME FRONT

The house in Bishops Avenue was always filled with voices. The children were forever having school chums over to play, and if they made more than their fair share of noise, it simply proved they were enjoying themselves. Freddie and I shared the belief that a house without voices is just an empty building. I often threw the doors open to play hostess to WIZO functions of various kinds which filled our home with scores of guests. Freddie never complained and always joined in with genuine enthusiasm. His natural bonhomie turned every occasion into a party.

But in June 1967 something occurred which saw the house transformed into the nerve centre of a hectic yet thrilling relief operation. In the preceding months there had been a great deal of warmongering among Israel's Arab neighbours. Syria intensified its bombardment from the Golan Heights. Egypt's Nasser forced United Nations peacekeepers out of Sinai and the Gaza Strip. There was a rare moment of unity among the Arab states and they began predicting that Israel would be crushed like a nut in their jaws. Then Egypt moved crack troops up to the Sinai border. The scene was set for open war.

The one element that the Arab axis had overlooked was the strategic genius of Israel's Defence Minister, Moshe Dayan, hero of the 1956 War. He was a firm believer in the adage that attack is the best means of defence. So at 7.45 in the morning of June 5, 1967, he struck out simultaneously against the Syrians, the Jordanians and the Egyptians. So began the Six Day War. The first stage was a series of air raids which reduced the enemy airfields to craters and destroyed their MIG fighters and bombers on the ground.

Israeli troops then stormed into Sinai, driving the Egyptians right back to the Suez Canal. The current joke in Britain was: "Come to Israel and see the pyramids." In the east the advancing Jordanians were routed on the banks of the Jordan, and in the north, the Syrians were flushed out of the Golan Heights. Jordan's King Hussein gave in on the third day. By day six, Egypt and Syria had also capitulated. Israel's triumph was one of the greatest offensive coups the world has ever witnessed. But like all these things, it came at a cost.

Israeli paratroops were still in the thick of battle when the first SOS call came to our Hampstead home. It was a highly-placed friend in Israel. He got straight to the point. "Susi, we need help."

"What kind of help?" I asked.

"*Every* kind of help."

But what it came down to was that Israel was suffering dire shortages in all sorts of fields and needed fresh supplies urgently. I immediately shelved all my WIZO commitments to take on this new challenge. The first thing I did was to press gang Paula and a dozen of my closest friends to man the phones right round the clock. There were three phones in the house and they never stopped ringing. Even the line which carried our burglar alarm was pressed into service. But whatever the time, there was always someone there to answer – Miriam, Esther, Joy, Jill, Sara, Audrey, and all the others. Each one stayed by the phones until other responsibilities, such as home and children, took precedence. The atmosphere was very fraught but we were all pulling together, and my friends were magnificent. The priority was to find out exactly what was needed. After that, I would ring around my contacts until someone came up with the goods.

Among the early demands was a call for 50,000 sweaters. They were needed for the soldiers fighting in the Sinai, because at night the desert is bitterly cold, even in high summer. There was one proviso: the sweaters had to be in dark shades. After all, one could not have front-line troops sporting bright red or yellow sweaters. This was an easy one. I phoned Cecil Gee's, the men's fashion chain, and told them: "You get them for us and have them dyed, and we'll parachute them over the desert." In just two days that's precisely what we did. My brother-in-law, Ernie, chartered a plane and had the sweaters delivered to the Sinai. Those Israeli desert troops were the best dressed soldiers ever to go to war.

The biggest need was for medical supplies. In these first hours of fighting there was a very real fear that Israel's losses might be immense. It did not seem possible that we could take on such heavily-armed foes without a terrible sacrifice, therefore our efforts in Hampstead were imbued with a real sense of urgency. Within a matter of days, I had managed to get hold of six field hospitals, equipped with theatre lights, drips, operating tables, the entire paraphernalia. Freddie's friends chartered a ship, renamed it the SS Miriam, and five days after it sailed from the Pool of London, its vital supplies were being off-loaded in Haifa.

The Miriam also carried many, many tons of supplies which were too heavy to transport by air. Freddie rounded up dozens of eager recruits, boys from Jews' College, to load the cargo. They had not finished packing and it was Friday afternoon, but it would not have been right for Orthodox boys to continue toiling during the Shabbos. Freddie sent them home, though they were more than a little reluctant. Their places were taken by other willing hands, boys from Habonim, a non-religious Zionist organisation.

In the first days, as word of our successes spread, the phone lines became swamped. I had many good friends in Tel Aviv, two who were high in government ministries. They started the rush. "Susi, we need blankets. As many as you can send." Or, "Susi, we're down to our last stocks of sterile dressings. What can you do?"

What my friends and I did was we wheedled and cajoled. Sometimes we did not have to try too hard, because generally in Britain there was tremendous sympathy for Israel's cause. I networked with charity groups throughout the country so that I could buy critically needed medical supplies. Almost without exception, the UK's pharmaceutical companies willingly donated or sold us what we wanted. Our shopping list ranged from hypodermic needles to cotton swabs, from morphine to scalpels. Only two firms, Johnson & Johnson and Smith & Nephew, refused to sell us what we needed. They did so after lengthy deliberation, obviously fearing that if they helped us, they would damage their standing in Arab markets. Even later, when I approached them again, pointing out that the medicines were required for the tens of thousands of Egyptian and Syrian prisoners-of-war, they still refused to accept our money. I kicked up a stink, but they had dug their heels in.

The first few days of our emergency effort passed in a blur. I caught a few hours of sleep here and there, otherwise we were on the go the whole time. Joy's mother, Mrs. Mautner kept us supplied with coffee and sandwiches and fruit, for there just wasn't time to sit down and have a proper meal.

Meanwhile, we were in a state of constant worry. All of us had good friends and relatives in Israel. The sheer momentum of Dayan's tactics and the war on three fronts meant that the news was very fragmented. There was not a clear picture of what was going on. We kept working and praying.

And then, after three days, a business friend of Freddie's got a message on his telex machine. It said in short that the Arab forces were losing the war on every front, and Israeli soldiers had reached the Wall in Jerusalem. There was no need to worry anymore. It is hard to express quite how euphoric we all felt at that moment. If we had had the time, we might have broken open the champagne and celebrated, but the phones kept on ringing, and the calls for our help became more and more elaborate. Army doctors warned that their reserves of plasma for blood transfusions were running dangerously low. So we set up a nationwide blood donor appeal, with centres in synagogue halls staffed by volunteer doctors, and soon the plasma was en route to Israel.

Gradually the full story of the War emerged. Even now it is hard to believe. Israel had gone into battle with a mere 264,000 troops, and most of them were reservists. Its armoured corps consisted of only 800 tanks. Ranged against them were 390,000 regular Arab troops, plus untold reservists, and 1,800 tanks. Yet in the first four days alone, Israel had smashed the 100,000-strong Egyptian Sinai Army and destroyed hundreds of Russian tanks. The Syrians had 1,000 men killed and another 5,000 taken prisoner in the battle for the Golan Heights.

But peace did not bring any respite from our efforts. There was however a brief lull after a couple of weeks. I paused and took stock of the frantic life I'd been leading. I had not had a proper night's sleep for weeks. Apart from one good meal, after we'd heard that the Israeli troops had reached the Wall, I'd survived on apples, oranges and cheese sandwiches. I felt I deserved a treat and I knew just what would recharge my batteries. I needed my hair done. For a few blissful hours I luxuriated in the salon as I was fussed over and pampered. And then it was back to work.

Now there were new demands to help the wounded men. Perhaps the most challenging was the call from an army surgeon who feared some of his patients would lose their sight unless they underwent a then novel operation. It was called a corneal graft. Frankly, I'd never heard of such a thing, but by chance a friend of mine knew exactly what the surgeon had in mind. She was an extremely wealthy American woman with interests in the US pharmaceutical company, Dow Corning. At that time they were the only people in the world who could supply the grafts. The mission to get them to Israel was almost as delicate as the operation itself.

First of all they were flown to Britain in the diplomatic bag. Freddie's brother, Ernie, was waiting at Heathrow to collect them. The one snag was he had to get them through British customs. The officers were baffled. What are they? Why have you got them? How much duty should be paid on them? Ernie spent an anxious hour while they tried to make up their minds.

We were in Hampstead, but every bit as anxious. For that very afternoon, Freddie and I were due to fly out to Israel with the grafts. We had very little time to spare and the surgeon had stressed it was vital he had them now.

At Heathrow Ernie patiently explained the whys and wherefores of corneal grafts, and he told the customs officers of the pressing urgency. They finally got the message. They sent Ernie – and his precious cargo – on his way with their blessing, but only after he signed an indemnity stating that if they later discovered duties should have been paid, he would pay them.

He raced back to us, we collected the grafts, and off we flew. As the El Al jet landed at Tel Aviv, an ambulance was waiting on the runway to greet us. The driver almost snatched the case from us; then the ambulance, its lights flashing, screamed off towards the Sheba Hospital. Within hours the surgeon was carrying out the first corneal graft operation ever performed in Israel.

While that was going on, Freddie and I were being feted like royalty. We had already been thanked scores of times on the phone for the help we had given during the course of the War, but now we were seeing this gratitude at first hand. It was no use our proclaiming that we had done no more than our duty. Still, I must admit this VIP treatment was absolutely wonderful after all those turbulent days. And I knew there was still much to be done.

The key focus now was tending to the wounded. Medical supplies had already been taken care of but many of the men in hospitals around Israel were without creature comforts. I approached Kurt Popper and also Fidelity Radio, asking them to donate transistor radios for the soldiers' bedside lockers. They responded with thousands and thousands of them. Then a health official told me he needed hundreds of watches. Not just ordinary watches, but ones with an automatic mechanism. (This was of course long before today's battery-powered timepieces.) The reason they had to be automatic was they were destined for soldiers who had lost arms. I contacted various companies, including Accurist, and they came up with just what the doctor ordered. My father-in-law volunteered to fly them to Israel. He was somewhat concerned however because we did not have Israeli customs clearance. I told him: "Just put them in your suitcase and pretend you are an ordinary tourist."

He was not challenged and he smuggled the watches through, phoning me that night from the hospital to report their safe delivery.

Through the efforts of the Hampstead Home Front, I made many, many friends in Israel, from all shades of the political spectrum. I am proud to say they are still my friends. Many years later, after Michael's wedding, we went back to Israel and threw a huge party on the roof terrace of our penthouse. It is not an exaggeration to say that half the Government was there as was Menachem Savidor, the Speaker of the Knesset, Yitzhak Modai, later to become Finance Minister, Benny Begin, whose father became Premier Menachem Begin, and extreme left-wing, extreme right-wing, and middle-of-the-road politicians. Among the waiters I had hired for the event was a former airman in the Israeli air force. He was utterly bemused at the sight of so many politicians of such bitterly opposing views, all enjoying themselves together under one roof. At one stage the young waiter came up to me and said: "Mrs. Bradfield, I would like to shake your hand as a friend. To get together all these people, I don't know what you have, but it is wonderful."

I was paid many tributes in my work for Israel, but that counts among the most treasured.

Perhaps I had better explain how we had come to know so many high-placed officials in Israel. Some people collect antiques, or rare books or fine wines. Freddie and I always collected friends, not by design. That was just the way it happened. It seemed the most natural thing in the world. And whenever we added another friend to our circle, he or she stayed there for life. We placed great store on our friendships and we always kept in touch.

Many years before, when Paula and I first came to England, our first really close friend was Esther, an Austrian girl who was a refugee just like we were. Through Esther, we became friendly with her sister, Sara. And when Sara married, it followed that we added her husband to our list of friends.

Sara's husband, Chaim Schreiber, was an outstanding man. Born in Lemberg in Poland, he came to Britain as a refugee with only his talent to support him. But such a talent. Chaim was a genius at woodworking. He knew how to bend it, shape it, fashion it into whatever he wanted. His skills soon came to the attention of the authorities, and when War broke out, Chaim joined that select band of civilians whose work was deemed vital to the War effort. While his friends were being conscripted into the Pioneer Corps, he was singled out to join the Ministry of Supply under Lord Beaverbrook. Chaim was detailed to work on aircraft design. If this sounds a strange post for a woodworker, it must be remembered that most British aircraft of the time, notably the Hurricane and the Mosquito fighters, had wooden airframes. Chaim was later closely involved with research and development on gliders. The vast armada of gliders which bore tens of thousands of paratroops into Normandy on D-Day owed not a little of their design to Chaim Schreiber's genius.

After the War, he turned his talents towards consumer goods. He evolved a way of laminating several layers of wood, so that it could be curved almost as easily as plastic. His development gave us the first television cabinets. Had it not been for him, they would have been plain square boxes.

Chaim was later to use his knowhow to produce the first-ever fitted kitchens, and then bedrooms and lounge units. His company is still the market leader in its field.

He and Sara, as I said, were close friends, and, in the mid-fifties they invited Freddie and me to Tel Aviv for the Bar Mitzvah of their son, David. It was our first time in Israel and we were overwhelmed by the sheer hospitality of everyone we met. Within a day or two, the programme for our stay was filled to overflowing. Lunch here, afternoon tea there, supper somewhere else. And when we weren't off visiting the homes of friends, others were stopping by our hotel suite for a chat. Our visit was one hectic social whirl. We returned to Britain in need of a holiday, but with a whole host of new friends, particularly Kalman and Bila Rappaport, who seemed to know absolutely everyone. (They remain my closest friends in Israel.)

Israel rapidly became our favourite summer playground. We stayed at first in the Sharon, then the only hotel at Herzliyah, the beach resort a few miles from Tel Aviv. Later, when they built the Accadia hotel, we rested there. But we did not get much rest. Every visit followed the same pattern of parties and receptions. If Freddie and I stayed only a week, we did not have a minute to ourselves. If we were in Israel for a fortnight, we usually managed to squeeze in one day when we just basked on the beach and recharged our batteries.

Otherwise the pace was beyond belief. Everyone insisted we just had to visit them. It seemed rude to refuse such kindness, so we accepted as many invitations as was humanly possible. That often led to the crazy situation of Freddie and I eating three meals in a single evening, beginning with high tea, then a full-scale dinner, followed by a hearty supper. Our hosts' generosity was boundless, and even though food was not so plentiful then, they went out of their way to provide a veritable banquet for us. The tables were piled high with chicken, *tcholent* bean bake, aubergine salads, houmus, tehinah and pitta bread. One had to eat these dishes which had been lovingly prepared. Freddie and I always did our best then, after a few hours we would excuse ourselves and go off elsewhere to be greeted by another sumptuous repast.

Around the dinner tables, fierce arguments raged. Most of our friends held Likud right-of-centre political beliefs, but they still found ample grounds for disagreement. There were times when passions became so inflamed that one felt certain they would lead to violence. But somehow, under the influence of good food and a modicum of wine, everyone's temper was restored and the evening always ended in laughter and affection. Freddie and I thrilled to this vibrant society. It seemed as if the very pulse of Israel throbbed through those lively evenings. Indeed, the conversation and the company was so fascinating that sometimes we did not return to our hotel until two in the morning, by which time we were so tired we were like zombies. We used to kick our shoes off and just collapse fully-dressed on to the bed.

In the morning, over a rather late breakfast, Freddie and I would discuss the evening before. Inevitably, we had met yet more new acquaintances and they had added their invitations to the growing pile in our suite. Looking back, I believe that everyone felt a *need* to forge new friendships. All of us had lost loved ones in the Holocaust and this desire to build acquaintances was, I suppose, a subconscious desire to fill that unfillable vacuum. There was too the sense that Israel was a young and vulnerable state. It needed all the friends it could get.

The people we met were of a similar age and background. They were all successful yet still ambitious. Years later, many of those who traded insults around the dinner tables would become respected statesmen and international businessmen. Nowadays they have a gravitas, a solid respectability. The one thing that has not changed is they remain true friends.

Naturally, while we were in Israel, we did our best to reciprocate the lavish hospitality by inviting people to our suite. This had drawbacks, in that we could never invite as many as we wanted, plus it effectively more than doubled the cost of our stay. The only solution was to buy our own apartment where we could entertain at will. It also helped us trim our waistlines by cutting out those three-dinners-a-night evenings.

A FITTING MEMORIAL

In the 'Seventies, while I was splitting my time between raising Michael and Cherry and my work with WIZO, Freddie was equally busy.

Bradfield, Brett & Co. was now under the Reed International umbrella, and both Freddie and Paul were on the board of the parent company. Ernie had chosen to go his own way, at least for a time. But that changed when he met a mutual friend in Philadelphia who had a thriving business in hospital insurance.

The idea appealed to Ernie, and on his return to Britain he got together with his brothers and told them of it. They too saw the potential, because many people faced real hardship when they became ill. The State sickness benefit was not sufficient to feed the family if the breadwinner was off work for any length of time. Now, under the hospital insurance scheme, people could buy cover for only a modest outlay.

Freddie and Paul resigned from Reed International, and, together again, the brothers launched Hospital Plan Insurance Services. Like everything else they had ever put their talents to, it was a tremendous success.

Each of the three had different abilities which complemented the others. Freddie was a gifted administrator, Ernie was the ideas man, and Paul was very adept at the day-to-day running. The business was split three ways, with each as an equal partner. But it was soon to add a fourth.

Even as a small boy, Michael styled himself "Junior" and modelled himself on his father. With his little toolbox in his hand, he would follow Freddie around the house, saying, "Dad, I want to work with you."

As he grew up, he never for one moment deviated from his game plan. At the Hasmonean grammar school – where, incidentally he notched, up a brilliant academic record that had his teachers reaching for superlatives – Michael began to display his father's keen eye for business. He augmented his pocket money selling sweets and comics to fellow pupils.

March 1989: On the terrace of our St. John's Wood home, Freddie and I prepare to welcome guests to yet another party.

After grammar school he studied economics for a year at Tel Aviv University, and completed his degree at the London School of Economics, where he achieved a Second. By rights it should have been a First with Honours, but when he was supposed to be swotting up for his finals, Michael was channelling all his energies into computers. They were then relatively new-fangled, but he quickly grasped how important a role they would play in all our lives. He studied them in his spare time and it soon became apparent that he had an uncommon flair. Economics rather went by the board and he rapidly emerged as one of the country's leading computer experts.

Freddie and his brothers saw Michael's expertise as something which could put their business in the forefront of the technological revolution, and in 1972 he fulfilled his dream of working alongside his Dad. He was immensely proud, as was Freddie. Michael's computer knowledge soon became invaluable to the business and it was so appreciated by the three brothers that they made him the fourth partner, sharing equally in the company's success.

Ernie and Paul were more than happy with the arrangement. They saw Michael's involvement as a bridge between the generations. Ernie's son, George, and Paul's son, Edward, were both only little boys at the time. But their fathers hoped they would emulate Michael and join the family business. And that's what they did.

Freddie never retired, though he did begin to take things slightly easier. We began to have more time for holidays. He was an enthusiastic skier, and, away from the winter sports season, he always loved going to Israel. But he was not terribly keen on staying in hotels – they curbed his zest for entertaining – which is why we ended up having apartments in Israel and Switzerland.

❖ ❖ ❖

Freddie died in 1991. I lost not only my husband but my best friend. My children and grandchildren lost a wonderful man who loved each of them very deeply.

Shortly before he died there was a curious incident. He was at services in the synagogue when he got called up for an *Aliya*. Normally, in a large synagogue such as ours, a man is told well in advance if he is to be called up. But this happened quite out of the blue at Succot. Freddie was taken aback, but of course he was pleased that he had received the honour of the *Aliya*. He was still a shade bemused after the service and he said to me: "I wonder what brought that on."

My first memorial to Freddie was a clinic in his name for new immigrants at Nahal-Beka. It was a proud moment too for Michael and Cherry. On the left is my cousin, Israel Shilat.

He died only a few days later. Some time afterwards, I asked the Rabbi why he had chosen that particular time to call Freddie up. He said: "It's just something I've wanted to do."

I needed to have something permanent, something life-affirming in his memory. My intention was to name it after him but Michael and Cherry insisted it bore both our names, because we were always so close. I knew precisely what I wanted for Freddie, but it took me three years to make it a reality.

In the meantime Israel was undergoing a fresh welfare crisis with immigrant families in Beersheba, and I saw a way of helping and of having something there in Freddie's name. The once dusty desert outpost was now playing home to thousands of new immigrants, many of them from the old Soviet Union. On the outskirts of the city at Nahal-Beka a great township had sprung up in a matter of weeks. Some 12,000 people were housed in Portakabins. They had roofs over their heads and they had food. WIZO had provided creches and kindergartens, but the new citizens were desperately short of medical care.

Just after Passover in 1992, six months after his death, I opened the Fred Bradfield clinic in Nahal-Beka. I also donated three scanning machines in Freddie's name to the Beersheba clinic, of which the Nahal-Beka unit was a branch. The clinic opening was attended by more than 200 friends and several leading politicians, among them the then Minister for Housing, Ariel Sharon. Many of the VIP guests present had known Freddie personally and their attendance was as much to honour him as to celebrate the opening of a desperately needed clinic. Everyone was exceptionally kind and

The Nahal-Beka ceremony was attended by Cabinet Ministers, among them Ariel Sharon.

in their speeches they paid tribute to Freddie's generosity and humanity. But perhaps the sweetest tribute was a silent one, paid by a little immigrant boy of no more than five or six years old. In the midst of our celebratory luncheon, the boy darted out of the crowd, plucked a red carnation from the table decoration and presented it to me with a grave smile.

In November 1994, the long-planned Freddie and Susi Bradfield WIZO Centre opened in Jerusalem. It is a handsome, two-storey building with wide terraces and 5,000 square feet of space. Its rooms are in use 18 hours of every day, and the programme of activities that takes place there is rich and diverse. I am particularly proud of the support that the Centre gives to children with special needs. There is also ante-natal care, and post-natal care. There is special tuition to help schoolchildren with their homework. There are Hebrew courses for emigrants, and Bar Mitzvah and Bat Mitzvah classes. There are two kitchens, and one is given over to teaching children the importance of proper nutrition. They even cook their own well-balanced meals, standing on little stools so that they can stir the pots. Young housewives attend aerobics classes and there are many cultural activities reflecting the great diversity of our people. I know Freddie would have approved.

There are two aspects which I feel would have particularly delighted him. Sometimes the rooms echo to the music of a Russian fellowship group. Immigrants, carrying the precious balalaikas, violins and ukeleles they brought with them from the old Soviet Union, stage impromptu concerts which set everyone's toes tapping. The music may be very different, but the mood is the same as it was in Freddie's jam sessions.

The other point that would have thrilled him is that the Centre which bears his name is in an official guidebook, listing the most attractive new buildings in Jerusalem. As a frustrated architect, he would really have appreciated that.

Many, many people benefit from Freddie's legacy. But to me, his most important legacy is the family of which he was the head. Time and time again, I catch a certain look, a certain gesture from Michael or Cherry, and I am instantly reminded of their father. Sometimes it is there in his grandchildren.

Cherry, for example, inherited Freddie's organisational talents. Although she is quite slight of build, Cherry has always been fiercely independent. She has her father's artistic bent, which is why she chose to study film and television in a four-year course at Tel Aviv University. After that, she went backpacking around the world. Naturally I was constantly worried about the risks, but when Cherry makes her mind up to do something, she does it.

When she returned to Britain, she found film and television studios were a closed shop to anyone without an Equity card. So Cherry set about launching her own business. I'm not sure where she got the idea, but it was a winner. Her one-woman company produced painted basketware for gifts. Soon she had Harrods, Fortnum & Mason's and Liberty all calling her with orders. Her studio was in Brick Lane in the East End, a rather humble address for such an upmarket line. Cherry was now in her early twenties and did not have a serious boyfriend. Freddie and I were not worried. We knew Cherry could not be rushed into anything. When the right man came along, that would be that. What we didn't know was that it would take nothing less than an El Al strike before she found the right man.

Cherry wanted a week's holiday and she had her heart set on Israel, but because of the strike there were no flights between London and Tel Aviv. I suggested she fly to Athens and possibly she could make a connection there. She phoned me from Athens to say the flights were still grounded. But, she added, would I mind if she went instead to the Club Med resort in Corfu? I wasn't terribly keen on that, but I consented.

In Corfu, the Club Med people did their usual bit of matchmaking, seating Cherry at a table with two handsome young men and another woman of her age. The trio spoke together entirely in Hebrew, while Cherry, for reasons best known to herself pretended she did not understand the language. All through the evening, the young men talked of no-one but her, and in very flattering terms. Cherry simply ate her dinner in silence, never once betraying that she understood perfectly every word spoken. Then, at the end of the meal, she stood up and in fluent Hebrew said to the men: "Thank you for a very interesting evening. I've enjoyed your conversation." And off she flounced, leaving two deeply embarrassed young men and a giggling young woman.

That's how it all started. By the end of the week, Cherry and one of her admirers, Alberto, were inseparable. Nor was it merely a holiday romance. When she returned they phoned each other all the time. Eventually he came to London and we had our first look at the young man Cherry never stopped talking about.

Alberto had an aristocratic background, being the eighth generation of a family of Italian Jews. He was a very fine young man with great dignity. We all took to him at once. At that stage he was studying business administration at the Bar Ilan university in Israel.

He and Cherry wed the following July, when she was 24. They spent the first year of their marriage in America, where Alberto was studying for an MA at New York University, and afterwards, to my great surprise, they settled in Italy. I was always convinced they would make their home in Israel. But Alberto's parents, Mauricio and Lina Eman, ran a high quality manufacturing company in Milan, and being the only son he was keen to join the family business. Cherry took to her new surroundings with enthusiasm and all her innate organisational skills came to the fore. She became very active in knitting together Milan's Jewish community. She recruited a set of other young women to form the Russian Support Group which carries out sterling work for Jewish enclaves in the old Soviet Union. The Milan group has adopted Kherson, a Ukrainian settlement comprising more than a hundred thousand Jews.

Cherry's interest and involement in what used to be called the Soviet Union goes back to her school days in Hampstead when she joined the Thirtyfives, an aid group dedicated to easing the plight of persecuted Jews behind the Iron Curtain.

There were various ways in which one could help the group's activities, by fund raising, for example, or by taking part in protests to raise public awareness of the Soviet injustice. And that is how she started lending support, but Cherry, who was never one for half measures, was determined to find out for herself the situation in Russia.

Naturally we were not terribly keen on the idea. At the time, Leonid Brezhnev, a Communist of the old guard, was president and under his regime all forms of protest were ruthlessly quashed. The KGB systematically purged Jewish dissidents, sending them to the Gulag labour camps or locking them up as "psychiatric patients" in primitive mental institutions. In the West there was a constant clamouring for news of the prisoners and the only way information could be gathered was by going to Russia and speaking to the families of dissidents. That is precisely what Cherry resolved to do.

She and a group of friends masquerading as tourists flew to Moscow on what was ostensibly a sight-seeing trip. Her suitcases were crammed with state-of-the-art consumer products and an amazing number of pairs of Levis jeans. For a teenager, she also had a surprising amount of money in dollars. Somehow she convinced the Russian customs officers that all clothes and the money were for her own use. But the young people were in effect sumgglers and the consumer goods were their contraband. The plan was to exchange the dollars and sell their wares on the black market and give the money to the families of dissidents. They also had prayer books and the Pentateuch to share out among the Jewish community where they could be copied and used to practise their faith.

Cherry was in Moscow for ten days and I did not have a proper night's sleep the whole time. I imagine the other parents were just as stressed. It must be remembered that in those days foreign tourists immediately came under intense KGB surveillance as soon as they set foot on Russian soil. Their hotel rooms were bugged and they were followed everywhere. Any tourist caught dealing with black marketeers could expect summary arrest and an unpleasant stay in a Soviet prison. But black marketeering was a minor offence compared to contacting dissidents who were officially branded enemies of the State. Anyone found giving them aid faced a battery of charges, from subversion to spying. Even the act of passing on prayer books warranted heavy penalties. Some western Christians were already languishing in prison for smuggling bibles. Small wonder then that we parents were so concerned.

But Cherry and her friends returned, mission accomplished. She reported back that she had visited several families and learned first hand of the problems they faced. She also found out a great deal about the dissidents held without trial in the notorious Lubiyanka prison.

Even after the thrill of her Moscow adventure had died down, Cherry kept up a close interest in the Soviet states, and years afterwards she visited the Ukraine. By this time the old Communist empire was crumbling and it was easier to send support. And the Jewish community of Kherson certainly needed it. In her role with the Milan group, Cherry helped launch a school and the women organised container convoys of second-hand clothes to the Ukraine. Many of these were sold and the money used to pay the teachers' wages.

Her group is also active in her adopted city. Not very long ago Cherry and the team built a youth centre, *Mifgash*, in Milan which was officially opened by the then Italian Premier, Silvio Berlusconi. He took one look around the splendid centre and said ruefully: "I wish all our Italian young people had clubs like this."

Cherry is also a leading light in WIZO's Milan chapter, and, as if that weren't enough, she has two lively children to tend to. Marco was born in May 1988, and Miriel in November two years later. Miriel is an exact clone of her mother, always busy, always fiercely independent. Cherry hotly denies that Miriel takes after her: she blames *me* for Miriel's independent streak.

Michael's marriage also had its origins in a holiday romance. They say that the Hilton Hotel in Tel Aviv is the greatest matchmaker in the world, and it certainly proved true in his case.

Just after Passover in 1977, he was staying at the Hilton when he met Bettina, who came from Leeds. It's ironic to think that her home was only a few hours drive from ours in London, yet they had to go all the way to Tel Aviv to meet. They married the following year when Michael was 26 and Bettina 19. His bride was not only beautiful and intelligent. She is also a very talented cook and today she is much in demand as a party caterer.

Their first child, Gabrielle, was born in 1980, and Matthew came along seven years later. Sometimes as I observe the bond between father and son, I am reminded so much of how close Michael and Freddie were. The bond is just the same. Like his father before him, Matthew says: "I'm going to be exactly the same as my daddy, and when I'm grown up, I'll work with him."

Michael, like Cherry, is very active in the Jewish community. He places great stress on Jewish continuity through educating young people. This has led to his long and fruitful association with the Jerusalem College of Technology. It enrols only the most gifted students and teaches them computer sciences.

Some years back Michael became aware of the dreadful death toll on Israel's roads after some of his friends were killed in accidents. He resolved he must do something to end the carnage and he devised MEROM, a sophisticated computerised system for regulating traffic flow. The scheme was so revolutionary that it was featured on the BBC-TV programme *Tomorrow's World*, which highlights the brightest and best new inventions. It is now successfully in use in Israel, and a great many other countries are keen to adopt it. MEROM was initially financed by the family trust, but we made a gift of it to the Jerusalem College of Technology which will benefit from franchising the system around the world.

The formal opening of the Freddie and Susi Bradfield WIZO Centre in Jerusalem. The city's mayor, Ehud Olmert, greets Raya Jaglom, president of World WIZO, and its international chairwoman, Helen Glesser. My brother Siche is second on left.

THE LOCKED DOOR

Many of those who came through the Holocaust kept their memories locked inside them for the best part of 50 years. It was as if it had taken them that long to come to terms with what they had endured, what they had seen in the camps. Then slowly people began to speak of their experiences. That started a great process of catharsis, and at last the ghosts of the past were exorcised. There were books, films, TV documentaries, and the world finally learned the terrible details of what happened. Very often, a survivor's sons and daughters would be wholly oblivious of what their father or mother had gone through. The young found it hard to accept that their parents had endured so much and been silent so long.

This silence was endemic to my generation. One did not talk about the War because everyone had such a sad story to tell. We were all maimed by our losses. Forty years after the *Shoah*, Israel staged a reunion of those who had survived the camps. The celebrated sculptress Naomi Blake, who is a very close friend, quite suddenly said to me. "I must go to the reunion. I have to talk it out of my system."

This was the first time in our many years of friendship that I learned that Naomi had been in a concentration camp. She had survived Sobibor, but like the others, she had never spoken of her ordeal. Naomi's works often featured a mother protectively cradling an infant. Now I understood that this potent universal image was something etched on her mind in the camps.

Naomi attended the reunion and talked to others who had come through the same terror. It was only after she returned that she was able to speak openly about her experiences.

In every sphere of one's memory, one sealed off the past. Perhaps we were all in a state of denial, seeking to obliterate our pain and bereavement. There was even silence about the *Kindertransport*, because so many of those who escaped had left their mothers and fathers, friends and relations behind.

In Canons Park, north London, there is a remarkable woman called Bertha Leverton. She first came to England from Munich on the *Kindertransport* and she has made it her lifetime vocation to form an international network linking everyone who made that journey. On the 20th of June,1989, Bertha succeeded in staging a 50th anniversary reunion in London. All of us who had come across on the *Kindertransport* were invited to the two-day event at the Harrow Leisure Centre. I was not particularly keen to attend, largely because my memories of that grim journey were something I had been doing my best to forget. I remembered the fear, the uncertainty, the loneliness. I remembered too those who were not given a ticket to freedom. There were too many ghosts and I did not wish to disturb them. But Paula was eager to go and, with considerable reluctance, I agreed to go with her.

The anniversary began on what must have been the hottest day of the year, with temperatures in the high eighties. Even before we arrived I felt drained. As we reached the centre I could see scores of people flocking in through the doors. I was in no hurry to join them, and instead I sat down to rest on a shaded bench just around the corner. There was already another woman, a stranger, seated on the bench. For a long moment she looked searchingly into my face. Then she said: "You wouldn't be Susi, by any chance?"

I was too startled to speak. The woman reached into her handbag and pulled out a photograph of me as a little girl.

She said: "I am Erika."

Erika! A long-forgotten memory came back. The last time I had seen her was that first day in England, in the Jewish Temporary Shelter. Then we had exchanged photographs and promised to keep in touch. And now, out of the thousands of people attending the *Kindertransport* reunion, she was the first person I met. The coincidence of our meeting left me numb with shock. She told me that she was now living in America and working as a travel agent in New Jersey. She said: "I came all this way because I hoped I would see you again."

I listened to Erika's story of how she had fared in the intervening years, but I said very little because I was still too shaken.

We went into the hall which was laid out with scores of blue-covered tables, each carrying place cards. There were upwards of a thousand people already in the centre. They came from Israel, France, America and all the far countries of the world – including one man from Nepal. But the seating was arranged according to one's place of origin, so the *Kindertransport* group which left Vienna was placed here, the Berlin contingent there, the Frankfurt refugees over there, and so on. Paula and I found our places. The faces around us were unfamiliar, yet some of them I must have known. Every now and then someone would thread through the tables carrying a placard on which was written the date of one particular *Kindertransport* departure. This was the signal for all those who travelled on that train to group together. Eventually I saw the sign *Berlin: January 18th, 1939.* That was the day we said goodbye to Berlin. We rallied round the placard and met our fellow travellers, but again there was no one I recognised. This is hardly surprising. Our sole point of contact was a nightmare 30-hour journey by train and ferry, a journey filled with tears and heartbreak. Now being here with all these people brought back the trauma. It took me some time to come to terms with it.

The ceremony was officially opened by Timothy Renton, the British Home Office minister. He spoke at some length about how proud he felt to be able to address us. I reflected that he was representing the very same Government department which had done its best to block refugees entering Britain. Princess Diana sent her greetings and various speakers paid tribute to the *Kinder*, stressing that Germany's loss was the free world's gain. And indeed, our small community of refugees had produced some outstanding citizens, among them the internationally-renowned immunologist, Leslie Brent, and the celebrated sculptor, Frank Meisler.

Quite a few who had arrived on the shores of England with nothing but a favourite toy and a change of clothes were now millionaires. They were naturally on top of the world, for this reunion reminded them how they had triumphed over adversity.

The gathering had attracted a great deal of media interest and I found myself being interviewed by a reporter from Berlin's main radio station. He asked me for my memories of the journey, and for the first time in 50 years I spilled it all out. I had never even told my children these things. As I talked I saw again the black uniforms of the Gestapo, the distraught children on the platform, the parents who were soon to die. It was a long interview and when it was over I felt utterly limp and lifeless. These were memories I did not want to awaken. They were too vivid, too unhappy. I know that many people found the reunion therapeutic in that they were able to talk openly. But for me it opened a door in my mind that I had wisely kept locked for 50 years.

Nor did I feel a common bond with the reunited *Kindertransport* refugees. Our lives before the journey were unconnected, and after our arrival in England we had each gone our separate ways.

On the walls of the centre were long lines of photographs depicting the thousands of children as they arrived off the boat. Many of the photos resembled the end-of-term school snaps in everyone's family albums. Yet these children were different. When one looked into their faces one saw fear and loneliness reflected in their eyes. Only a few managed a brave smile for the camera. We found the photograph of Paula and me, two frightened little girls a long way from home. I remembered how I had rehearsed my first words in English: *"My name is Susi. I am nine. I am from Berlin."*

Along the walls at the reunion others crowded to stare into the black and white photographs and confront their past. I turned away, for this was something I did not wish to confront.

At the time they fled, many of the children on the *Kindertransport* were too young to understand what was happening to them. Now, as adults, they found they did not even have a memory of that journey. Here at the reunion they went from group to group, filling in the gaps in their personal history. I have no doubt that the occasion helped a great number of people. They felt perhaps that by talking to each other they shared the burden of the past. Some of the meetings were openly joyous.

Many refugees had gone on to become industrialists, doctors, artists, successful businessmen, and they saw the *Kindertransport* as their deliverance.

But on the second day of the reunion, we heard stories with deeply unhappy endings. One after another, speakers went up to the flower-bedecked rostrum and told their harrowing tales. Some, especially the very young children, had been placed with non-Jewish families and had lost their birthright, their identity. Others spoke of how they had been forced to slave in an unloving household. Some were brutally abused. They told their stories with tears coursing down their cheeks. Their anguish was too much to bear. I left mid-way through the second day for I just could not take any more.

I was reminded quite forcibly of just how fortunate Paula and I had been. We had never had to slave or cower in our adopted homes in England. We were always loved and cared for by our foster parents. And even more important, we were given back our own parents. How then could I possibly identify with these people who had lost everything? Their stories deeply distressed me for I had been given so much. Yes, we had lost our grandparents and relatives and friends. But weighed in the balance, these other *Kindertransport* veterans had lost infinitely more. I felt almost as if I did not have the right to be there to share their suffering.

I came away from the reunion in a mood of utter melancholy and it took me many weeks to shake myself free of it. I think I was trying to rationalise the lottery that life is. And while I was thinking along these lines, phrases from our most holy prayer, on the Day of Atonement, sprang to mind:

How many shall pass away, and how many shall be born, who shall live, and who shall die, who at the measure of man's days, and who before it...

I felt very keenly that I had been spared for a purpose. If you are singled out to live, then you have obligations to the living. The thought was very clear in my head. I believed that I was fulfilling my responsibilities through my work with WIZO. Even so, I still felt there was something *more* to be done. And it was then that I conceived of this book, for this is a story which must be told.

I nurtured the idea for several years, but there always seemed to be too many other things to do, so many other responsibilities to fulfill. The book lay unwritten.

It might have remained that way but for a singularly chance occurence.

I was in Israel and visiting the Holocaust museum at Yad Vashem where they had just opened the pavillion in memory of the one-and-a-half million children who perished. Its design is appropriately simple. One enters the domed circular building via a concrete ramp. Inside, the walls are dark and plain, but one's eyes are instantly caught by thousands and thousands of little flickering points of light across the dome. A single candle and a system of lenses and mirrors create the startling effect. Each tiny light symbolises a child whose life was taken.

While the visitor stands in silence under the flickering dome, a continuous tape recording, listing the name, the age and the birthplace of every child we lost, is played through hidden speakers.

As I walked into the building, the tape relayed a girl's name, adding: "Nine years old, from Berlin."

I stood rooted to the spot.

All I could think of was my own voice echoing back down the long, long years:

My name is Susi. I am nine years old. I am from Berlin.

I lifted my eyes to the sky of the dome and gazed on the myriad twinkling lights.

I had been spared.

But some became stars.

Ilse Kohn, born 5 April 1929, Vienna, Austria. Last news through Red Cross came on Dec. 1939, after which she was taken to a concentration camp with her mother, grandmother, aunt and other relatives...

...and she became a star.

Photograph reprinted by kind permission of Ilse's cousin, Mrs. Helga Bellenger.